IN BLOOD,
FLOWERS
BLOOM

IN BLOOD, FLOWERS BLOOM

FLOWERS BLOOM

A World War II Story of Valor and
Forgiveness Across Generations

SAMANTHA BRESNAHAN

PUBLICAFFAIRS

New York

PublicAffairs
Hachette Book Group
1290 Avenue of the Americas, New York, NY 10104
www.publicaffairsbooks.com
@Public_Affairs

Printed in the United States of America

First Edition: April 2025

Published by PublicAffairs, an imprint of Hachette Book Group, Inc. The PublicAffairs
name and logo is a registered trademark of the Hachette Book Group.

The Hachette Speakers Bureau provides a wide range of authors for speaking events. To
find out more, go to hachettespeakersbureau.com or email HachetteSpeakers@hbgusa.com.

PublicAffairs books may be purchased in bulk for business, educational, or promotional
use. For more information, please contact your local bookseller or the Hachette Book Group
Special Markets Department at special.markets@hbgusa.com.

The publisher is not responsible for websites (or their content) that are not owned by the
publisher.

Print book interior design by Bart Dawson.

Library of Congress Cataloging-in-Publication Data
Names: Bresnahan, Samantha, author.
Title: In blood, flowers bloom : a World War II story of valor and forgiveness across
    generations / Samantha Bresnahan.
Other titles: World War II story of valor and forgiveness across generations
Description: First edition. | New York : PublicAffairs, 2025. | Includes bibliographical
    references and index.
Identifiers: LCCN 2024035584 | ISBN 9781541702578 (hardcover) | ISBN
    9781541702868 (ebook)
Subjects: LCSH: Connor, Marty, 1926–2020. | Iwo Jima, Battle of, Japan,
    1945—Miscellanea. | Flags—Japan—History—20th century. | World
    War, 1939–1945—Trophies. | Cultural property—Repatriation—Japan. |
    Shiokawa, Masataka, 1944– | Wachi, Tsunezō, 1900–1990. | Soldiers—Family
    relationships—Japan. | United States. Marine Corps. Marine Regiment, 26th.
    Battalion, 1st—Biography. | Reconciliation—History.
Classification: LCC D767.99.I9 B747 2025 | DDC 940.540092—dc23/eng/20241219
LC record available at https://lccn.loc.gov/2024035584

ISBNs: 9781541702578 (hardcover), 9781541702868 (ebook)

LSC-C

Printing 1, 2025

To Patrick, for everything, forever.

CONTENTS

A NOTE ON NAMES

The main characters in this book are American and Japanese. Upon second reference, Americans are referred to by their first names, and Japanese by their family names, in keeping with Japanese tradition. In some sections where multiple people share the same Japanese surname, first names are used instead for clarification, or because of their own personal preference. Any derogatory names or terms that appear in the text are quoted from original material.

PROLOGUE

HIROSHIMA STATION, JAPAN / MARCH 13, 2023

The train pulls away from the station at exactly 8:22 a.m., as scheduled. Japan's high-speed shinkansen network knows no other way. I'm in car 6, seat 14B, next to my husband, on the Sakura-line train bound for Kurume, a city of roughly three hundred thousand on Kyushu, the southernmost main island of Japan. I'd only learned of Kurume recently, in preparation for a moment I did not think would ever come.

Back home, it is Sunday evening, the time difference having changed overnight from fourteen hours to thirteen with the start of daylight saving time. It is March 13 on this train and March 12 in the United States, and the Academy Awards are about to begin, and it is also Selection Sunday for the NCAA basketball tournament. But on this sleek bullet train, I'm not thinking about either of those things, nor does it register that the small latte I ordered at the station had been significantly cooled by the chill on the open-air platform while we waited.

Instead, I hope that the man we're traveling to meet has not forgotten we're coming. Even if he did, Kurume is not a big place, and I'm sure we can track him down. I feel an uncharacteristic sense of peace that I usually do not possess in moments like this, when I'm more often dominated by stress and making a mental run-through of every possible scenario, most of which are worst-case. Today, it seems the third member of our travel party, Kozue—part translator, part research assistant, part friend, all godsend—has taken up that post. She realized she did not save the man's number in her phone, and now the call history has bumped it out in favor of more recent numbers. She should have confirmed, she said earlier on the platform as my coffee cooled, and she's sorry, and she'll call his son's office at 9:00 while we're on the train, which feels like a more respectable time to start cold-calling people on a Monday morning.

Yet I am not worried. Again, uncharacteristic. Perhaps it is because I have actively kept my expectations low for today, have anticipated at every turn that he would cancel on us, that—still living in a pandemic—one of us might get sick before we arrive at our destination. Or, simply, that he would change his mind.

This is not the first time we've tried to meet him. I've known about this man for more than twelve years now. By supplying a list of questions I'd wanted him to answer to a Tokyo-based colleague in 2011, I had, in a way, interviewed him from afar. I'd read the bulk of his memoir, translated from Japanese. I'd seen photos of him, and videos, in particular a documentary by NHK, Japan's national broadcaster, that followed him in 2004, and I'd read news articles using an imperfect internet browser translation.

But we had never met in person. And when Kozue had asked on my behalf in 2017 and then again a year later, both answers were the same, and a bit gruff, and rather final: *Thank you, but no, I am done talking about this.*

So I was at peace with the outcome, having had five years of practice in thinking this would not happen.

And yet.

We are on a train. He is supposed to pick us up at the station at 10:00. I feel hopeful and grateful to be here in this country, doing this work. This story is important. He is important. And our earlier visit to Hiroshima was a good reminder of what's at stake when we lose sight of the things that are most important.

Two days prior, my husband, Patrick, and I were on another train, the 8:29 a.m. Hikari 565 shinkansen from Kyoto Station bound for Hiroshima, in car 9, seats 16A and B, the last row. It was largely empty on a beautiful Saturday morning. The countryside flew by, as did the ride, and we arrived at 10:31. I felt anxious, and I was also looking forward to this visit. I would catch myself forgetting what we were about to see, and then would suddenly remember and sense the gravity of the day. In many ways, it did not feel real.

Our first impression was that Hiroshima could be any city in the world. The lack of traditional Japanese architecture was striking, especially after our having come straight from Kyoto. But soon I remembered why that was. We had made reservations at the Sheraton adjacent to the station, so we did not have to go far when the train arrived. It also meant we didn't have our bearings at all, that we had seen almost nothing of the city other than what passed by the train window. The station was huge and filled with people: international tour groups following guides hoisting colorful flags on poles, people in suits although it was a Saturday, individual tourists, and a large number of people wearing red. The Hiroshima Toyo Carp baseball team, which plays in Japan's professional league, hosted a uniform-unveiling event at the stadium that day, and the closest train stop was Hiroshima Station. The place was crawling with Carp fans, who wore hats and shirts bearing the red *C* logo that appeared to be a replica of the Cincinnati Reds' logo from Major League Baseball, the influence undeniable. America's pastime so beloved here in a place America had once demolished.

Our hotel room not yet ready, we left our luggage with the bellhop and tried but failed to prepare ourselves for the day ahead. Around noon, we exited one of Hiroshima's legendary streetcars at the A-Bomb Dome stop. That's the name: "A-Bomb Dome stop," and aptly so—it was right there, across the street.

The remains of the dome defied both logic and gravity. The structure had become a symbol of the city itself: how it was, improbably, still standing when everything else was incinerated the morning of August 6, 1945; how it was, impossibly, still standing today, almost eighty years later, a shell of its former self. Bits of exposed rebar lurched midair, grasping at nothing. Are those dark stains scorch marks, or dirt in need of a pressure wash? We assumed the former, which is to say, the worst.

I felt sad and overwhelmed. I tried not to cry; that seemed like too much too soon. But then I'm not sure there was any right or wrong way to feel. We had come there, after all, to feel. Haunted, frightened, humbled. We spent some time taking in the building from all sides. Another couple sat just behind us, along the water's edge, eating lunch in the incomplete shadow of the hollowed-out dome. Everything was made all the more jarring as it was a picturesque day worthy of a postcard photo shoot.

We crossed a small bridge over the river to the other side of Peace Park and made our way to the memorial museum. We passed the eternal flame and then the arched monument with the names of the victims, designed in the shape of a traditional burial mound. A large Japanese flag on a white flagpole flickered in the breeze at permanent half-staff.

A small crowd had gathered in front of the memorial, each person taking their turn to get up close. We offered 500 Japanese yen into a little box and stepped forward to pay our respects. Guilt crept in around the edges of my consciousness as those waiting their turn behind us watched.

Yes, we are Americans, I wanted to say. Yes, we know. Yes, we feel sorry.[1]

Yes. Yes. Yes.

Behind us loomed the museum, with an adult admission fee of 200 Japanese yen ($1.47) each. The museum was daunting—dark and intense and also beautiful. I felt my brain trying to distance itself from the exhibits, speeding through the placards, the photos, seeing but not seeing. I had to force myself to slow down, return to the present.

We spied some mentions of Korean conscriptions and victims, including American prisoners of war, and a few points on Japan's entry into the war, even one brief mention of the Nanjing Massacre in the last section, on the history of Hiroshima, but if you blinked you'd miss it. A section was dedicated to the United

States' development and use of nuclear weapons. A plea for the end of nuclear arms: "No more Hiroshimas." There were many small children in the museum with their families. A sign before you entered said to keep an eye on their reactions. It was pain and horror and sadness. Images of human bodies ravaged beyond recognition. I remember being glad we hadn't eaten before our visit. The pictures were harrowing. Charred flesh and blistered skin. Dead bodies. Torn and burned clothing in tatters. It seemed impossible to imagine the being that wore them. So many kids' clothes. A tiny rusted tricycle. The preserved steps from outside a bank, a human shadow seared into the stone. The before-and-after of the city. Even seeing it, my brain could not comprehend. It was warm in there, which did not help. The feeling of guilt worsened; our anxiety levels rose. My KN95 mask, still strongly recommended to wear in public during the COVID-19 pandemic in Japan, felt hot and claustrophobic.

We spent roughly an hour inside. Afterward, we sat on a bench in the shade just beyond the exit doors, listening to trees in the breeze, decompressing. Patrick disassociated by looking at his phone. I wrote the notes that would become this Prologue. It was 1:41 p.m. The weather was almost unbearably nice considering our surroundings. My smartwatch said it was 69 degrees. There was a haze on the horizon but no clouds.

Before we left, I took a lap through the small gift shop. On impulse, I purchased a little porcelain, origami-shaped crane. I suppose buying it was about the message of peace and the reminder of what we are capable of doing to each other. I can't otherwise explain my need to commemorate being there, but making the purchase felt important in the moment—my own souvenir of a macabre event.

Outside the train window on Monday morning, Hiroshima behind us as we continue speeding south down the spine of Japan, we cross through some of the country's forty-seven prefectures, passing what look like industrial areas, until we're in Fukuoka, the prefecture that houses Kurume. Then we're at the station, which is much smaller and quieter than Hiroshima's massive transit hub, from which we had departed less than two hours before.

Kozue is on her cell phone, and I can pick out a few words—hai (yes), arigato gozaimasu (thank you)—and two names, Martin Connor-san, the man who started this, and Shiokawa-san, the one we've come all this way to see. I try to gauge Kozue's demeanor: positive and hopeful, or disappointed and worried, but I cannot quite read her. After a few moments, she hangs up. "That was his son's office," she says. "They are going to tell him to call me." We mill around in the arrival area of the train station. A breeze comes through, warmer than in Hiroshima; the southern air has a slight humidity.

Kozue's phone rings.

I hear the same words, minus Shiokawa-san, his name, and hope that means it's him on the other end. Again I cannot tell how it's going. She hangs up.

"He forgot we were coming," she says. "But he's on his way."

PART 1

CHAPTER 1

LEYTE, PHILIPPINES / LATE 1944

Lieutenant Jinichi Kodama was in trouble.

The odds were not in his favor, and surely he knew it. Since the Americans had arrived in Leyte just over a month before, in October, the number of men in Kodama's 16th Division of the Imperial Japanese Army had been decimated from eighteen thousand to just fifteen hundred.[1]

In the eyes of the empire, Kodama and his men were expendable, a means to a bloody end against a hated enemy force. A sea of uniformity, the Japanese soldiers were outfitted in the same drab olive uniforms, identical canteens swinging from straps, pouches hanging from belts, steel helmets lined with leather resting atop their heads. But each was a man, not a machine, and it was the personal things he carried that made him so: photos of loved ones, the corners peeling in the humidity; letters from home, signed with love; senninbari (thousand-stitch belt), a strip of cloth to be worn in battle for luck; and for many, a personalized Hinomaru, more commonly known as the Japanese battle flag. Signed by family and friends in the soldiers' home villages or cities, it was a physical representation of what they were fighting for. In Leyte, Jinichi Kodama had his.

But on December 8, 1944, in one final stand against the Americans, Kodama is believed to have suffered the same fate as so many of his men: killed during the defense of airstrips at Burauen. Back home in Fukui, a coastal city on the Sea of Japan, he'd left behind a wife and baby boy. His young son would not survive beyond the war; his wife would eventually leave the family; his parents would be killed in an air raid. His two siblings would be adopted by another family and would take the surname Sasaki. The Kodama family name was all but erased.

Yet it remained in one place: inscribed on the flag Jinichi had carried into battle, which was now in the possession of a US Army soldier named Arthur Pim, headed for the homeland of the enemy.

CHAPTER 2

Shannon Moore wasn't sure what she was doing there. For every box she removed, her mom put another in its place. But her mother had said she wanted help decluttering, so there Shannon was, muddling through dusty boxes in the backyard shed of her mom's home, just outside Buffalo.

The two-story, shingled shed was painted the same gray-blue as the house. Warmed by the summer sun, the shed's interior carried a musty smell, hinting at how long some of the boxes and their contents had been there.[1] Yet Shannon soon found herself enjoying this treasure hunt of sorts, uncovering relics from her mother's past.

In one box, she found a Bible from her parents' wedding, its white-lace cover partially stained with black soot from a house fire that had happened in the 1980s; in another, a centerpiece with a green speckled vase and faded white plastic flowers sat protected by crinkled sheets of newspaper. Then she spotted something unusual, the hard, metal edges out of place among the softness of her mother's possessions.

Shannon cleared the area to reach the small locker. Her mom confirmed it had belonged to Shannon's father, Arthur Pim, a US Army veteran of the Second World War. Arthur had died in 1975, when Shannon was only ten years old. Immediately she was drawn to the box, excited for anything that could connect her to her father, providing insight into the life of a man she had lost too soon.

Carefully, Shannon opened the locker. Bits of rusty screws, an old wooden pipe, and some jagged pieces of metal had settled inside, undisturbed for decades. There were stray seashells. *Dad must have picked those up on the beaches in the Pacific*, Shannon thought. Her eyes slid over every item in the box, settling on a balled-up old rag nestled between two jars. With her thumb and index finger, Shannon plucked it out of the locker and turned to throw it away in disgust.

Arm outstretched, hand hovering over the garbage can, she stopped. Something was telling her not to let go; instead, she gingerly pulled the fabric apart. The clumped ball of silk unfurled before her, transforming into an off-white rectangle. A large red circle emanated from the center. Around it, black strokes of ink became Japanese characters, their edges bleeding into the fibers. The characters formed sentences that spread out around the red ball like rays from the sun.

Instantly, she knew. This was not trash, or even an old handkerchief, or a discarded fragment of torn silk. It was a flag, and it could have come from only one place. Perhaps this piece of her father's life—a piece he'd kept mostly hidden—could provide clues and a connection to a man she longed to understand. After all, if the flag was still there, tucked away among other trinkets from his time in the military, it surely meant something.

It must.

It may be one of the most recognizable national symbols anywhere in the world. Striking in its simplicity, it leaves no doubt: the vibrant red circle on the white background is Japan's national flag.

The disk's resemblance to a fiery sun is no accident. Often called the Land of the Rising Sun, the country was led by an imperial dynasty founded in the seventh century BC by the Shintō sun goddess, Amaterasu, according to Japanese tradition.[2] Japan's emperors are all descendants of her grandson, the first ruler of Japan; still today, the emperor is known as the Son of the Sun as part of an unbroken imperial bloodline.[3]

Oral traditions of a "sun flag" date back centuries, but the current iteration was formally adopted on August 5, 1854.[4] Officially titled the Nisshōki (flag of the sun), it is commonly called the Hinomaru (circle of the sun) throughout Japan.[5]

A second flag, known as the Kyokujitsu-ki (rising sun flag), added sixteen red rays emanating from the sun. It rose to prominence around the early twentieth century, when Japan began its imperial takeovers in Korea.[6] Both versions are widely associated with the country during World War II, especially the Kyokujitsu-ki, which was an official symbol of Japan's military forces.[7]

Yet it was the Hinomaru that would take another, more personal form.

By tradition, Japanese soldiers carried a Hinomaru into battle, often carefully folded beneath their uniforms or tucked into a pocket. It was inscribed with good wishes from family and friends. The sixteen red rays of the military flag were replaced with the inked calligraphy of Japanese characters, emanating outward but, in keeping with tradition, not touching the sacred red circle.

The flags were made of silk—a new, military-forward use for what had become a burgeoning luxury industry.[8] But as the war progressed, silk production was shifted to manufacturing parachutes, and cheaper cotton cloth was sometimes used for the flags.[9] Some of the flags had tabs on the corners for reinforcement, made of leather when the material was available.

One flag carried by a soldier in Burma in 1945 included phrases such as "wishing you health victory," "invincible loyalty," and "long-lasting fortune for warriors," which, along with wartime slogans, were common sentiments. Most flags typically had the recipient's name inscribed along one side.

The flags were among the most intimate and literal representations of what Japan's soldiers were fighting for: country, family, honor. And they also became some of the most prized souvenirs removed from the battlefields of the Pacific.

Taking the spoils of war was not unique to the Pacific Theater of the Second World War; it was a practice that had been followed by victors in battle for centuries. But souvenir hunting in the Pacific during the 1940s reached an elevated level. At the center were the flags.

Along with other battlefield trophies—such as photos, diaries, thousand-stitch belts, and swords—the Hinomaru, in the hands of American, British, or Australian troops, moved into a new phase of existence, transforming from one spiritual meaning to another as it passed ownership: once given, now taken.

But for some of those flags, there awaited a third phase, an unexpected path that would bring the Hinomaru back home.

Arthur James (Bud) Pim was in rare company from birth: he was born on February 29, 1920, a leap year. The youngest of six children and the only boy born to his father, Arthur, and mother, Lena, he grew up in Buffalo, New York. Artistic and left-handed, yet ambidextrous, Bud later fought in Leyte and Luzon, islands in the Philippines, during World War II.

Private Pim wrote often to his sister Bernice (who had a nickname of her own, Babe), filling sheets of military-issued V-Mail

Arthur (Bud) Pim
(courtesy Shannon Moore)

with his slanted cursive.[10] He signed off frequently with "give my regards to the gang—love to all, Bud," and thanked his sister for writing with updates of the family. He constantly asked how the rest of his sisters were faring, or he told them about his Christmas turkey dinner in 1944, or he simply gave updates on the weather, imagining the snow back home in western New York.

"Well Babe the rainy season is back again," he wrote on March 14, 1945. "It's rained now for about a week straight so you can imagine how it is here." Two weeks later, he asked her if she'd save him "a taste of maple syrup."

He clung to his memories of home as the war raged around him. In the Battle of Leyte Gulf alone, more than twenty-three thousand American soldiers and sailors were killed.[11] Arthur Pim survived.

Bud returned to America, and thirteen years after the war ended, on November 15, 1958, he married Audrey Roll. The pair would have five children, including Shannon, raising the family in a modest home in the Buffalo suburb of Depew.

Shannon's early childhood featured plenty of family gatherings during the summer and an annual "family fun day" on the shores of Lake Erie at Crystal Beach over the Canadian border in Ontario. But some of her favorite memories involved Christmas, as "Santa was very generous" to what she considered the "quintessential family of the late sixties and early seventies."

On the surface, her father, by then employed as a freight conductor on the Erie Railroad before he was forced into early retirement by heart disease, enjoyed painting, cooking his signature spaghetti sauce, and whipping up oxtail soup. His young daughter knew very little of the war, or his role in it, or how it might have weighed on his mind, or why he had hidden away certain items in his old army locker.

All Shannon knew was that he loved her, and she him, and she delighted in his nickname for her: Shannon Boo, which he called out to her in a singsong way: "Shannon Boo, I love you!"

Arthur died in 1975, four days shy of his fifty-fifth birthday, and whatever feelings or secrets he held about the war went with him to the grave. Shannon was left behind to pick up the pieces of his story, to navigate the crossroads of a heavy decision, left to wonder if he, too, before he picked up the flag in the Philippines, felt the weight of his choice.

Arthur Pim and his
daughter Shannon
(courtesy Shannon Moore)

In the shed, Shannon turned around, holding the flag in front of her. "Your father must have brought that back from the war," her mother said, and told Shannon she could keep it.

Before the words had fully left her mom's lips, Shannon was halfway across the backyard. Tom, Shannon's husband, was in her mother's living room when he saw the delicate fabric in her hands. "That . . . that's a Japanese battle flag!" he stammered. To Shannon, he looked like a little kid on Christmas, eyes wide. Tom launched into the history of the flags, saying that almost all Japanese soldiers had them under their uniforms, and that American soldiers had brought them home as morbid souvenirs, often collecting their prize immediately after killing its original owner.

What Shannon knew about the war did not come from her father; he never spoke of it. She knew only that he had fought in the Philippines. She didn't know what war was like for him. She didn't know if he had seen death or killed anyone himself. She knew her dad to be a kind man with a loving smile. For all those years, he had kept his souvenirs, and his memories, tucked away in that army locker. The same locker had once sat in the basement, Shannon's mother told her, hidden behind some wood paneling, until a house fire in the 1980s forced everything out, and it ended up in the shed out back.

Now the flag was Shannon's. She delicately folded it up— "Careful!" Tom warned—and took it to their home nearby. She placed the folded fabric in the den, wondering what the Japanese characters could possibly say. But life took over before she could find out. With four children of her own, late summer soon became early fall, and it was time to go back to school.

Wrangling the kids took Shannon's mind away from the flag. For the second time in its existence, it faded into the background, resting untouched. And then Shannon's third-grade daughter, Sarah, approached her with an idea. It was November 2003, and Sarah needed to give a presentation for Veterans Day. Could she take the flag to school? "It's so cool," she said.

Shannon agreed, under two conditions: first, that they try to find out more about the flag's significance for the class presentation; second, that she be allowed to help. The last thing Shannon was going to do was send the fragile piece of fabric off to school with an eight-year-old. It had made it all the way to New York from the Philippines, from an old army locker into her life, and she wasn't going to lose it now.

Tom and Shannon sat together at the computer to begin their research. Lessons about Japanese battle flags filled the search results. They discovered that the inscriptions on the flag likely had been written by the fallen soldier's community—prayers and well-wishes to remind him of home. They read about American veterans around the country who'd started returning the flags to Japan, reuniting the treasures with families of the soldiers who had once carried them into battle. Shannon thought it was a beautiful idea. But she didn't quite know where to start.

She figured a good first step might be translating the writing on the flag. With Sarah and the flag in tow, she drove to the University at Buffalo, where a Japanese professor of linguistics, Mitsuaki Shimojo, deciphered the script.

Born in Osaka, Shimojo had come to the United States for his graduate studies. He had grown up hearing about the war from his parents, and had seen pictures of flags like this one, but had never seen one in person before. He was pleasantly surprised at how well preserved it was. He felt the history there in the room with them.[12]

He began reading the characters, every brushstroke a clue. "This belonged to a soldier named Jinichi Kodama," he said, and Shannon felt her heart pound. She began to realize the human connection behind the flag. It represented a person, a soldier, a life—just like her own father.

It's possible that Arthur Pim never came across Kodama himself; sometimes souvenirs were traded between GIs, or even stolen from them. It's possible someone else killed Kodama. It's possible he died from mortar fire and not during hand-to-hand combat. It's possible he never saw the face of the person responsible for his death.

It's also possible that he did.

At the university that day, a reporter and photographer from the *Buffalo News* stood off to the side of the room, observing. Sarah's school principal had called the paper to say there was something they might want to see.[13] On November 24, 2003, the *News* ran a story under the headline "History Hidden Away: Japanese Battle Flag Found amid Shed's Clutter."[14] Down I-90 in Syracuse, another journalist picked up the paper, and then he picked up the phone. Sean Kirst knew exactly who Shannon Moore needed to contact if she wanted to get that flag back to Japan and reunite it with Jinichi Kodama's family.[15]

She needed Marty Connor.

CHAPTER 3

PACIFIC OCEAN / FEBRUARY 1945

Something was strange. Marty Connor opened his eyes and waited until they adjusted to the darkness, listening. It was the engines; they were softer, they had slowed.[1] It was time.

Marty rolled off his cot and pushed through two heavy canvas curtains that served as doors. Out on the deck of the USS *Deuel*, he saw an island three, maybe four miles away. It was three in the morning. Under normal circumstances, he never would have seen the island from that distance, cloaked in the thick darkness at sea. But these were far from normal circumstances. The island was lit up, a scorching glow piercing the night. Bombers roared over Marty's head, peppering the mound rising from the water with rockets and napalm.

It was February 19, 1945. D-Day at Iwo Jima.

Marty watched the assault from the relative safety of his ship, then headed to breakfast. He joined his fellow Marines in the mess hall and picked up a metal tray. That morning, the mess cooks treated them to steak and eggs, a delicacy reserved only for those headed into combat. Too many men wedged on board meant no seats in the hall, so Marty stood at a table and savored his food. He had no idea how long it would be until he had another hot meal. He wondered if this would be the last meal for the guy on his left, on his right, for him. Everyone looked so young, and they were. Just eighteen, Marty should have been back home in Syracuse, preparing for college.

Marty finished breakfast and headed back to his bunk. He squared away his gear, double- and triple-checked his pack. He'd be landing on Iwo with his M1 rifle, ammunition, and two hand grenades, which clipped onto rings attached to the straps of his pack, near the shoulders. He put pieces of tape over the levers on the grenades; if he fell during the landing, he didn't need the pins coming out and detonating the grenades. Fighting the Japanese would be hard enough. No need to create his own danger.

In the top pocket of his utility jacket, Marty tucked away his little black prayer book. He wanted it close by.

The call came at around seven in the morning. Members of the Fifth Marine Division, 26th Regiment, 1st Battalion, began spilling over the side of the transport ship. Marty swung his leg over the rail and wedged a foot in the cargo net. The mantra from training repeated in his brain: feet in the horizontal, hands in the vertical.

He glanced down at the boat below him, gauging the sea. Rough waters could cause the boats to rise and fall as much as ten feet, making a dangerous operation even tougher. Marty was relieved. The seas were calm and cooperative. The boat sat in

Marty Connor
(courtesy Connor family)

place, waiting for him. Maybe it was a good sign. Maybe there was hope.

Thirty-six Marines formed three lines in what were called Higgins boats, amphibious transport ships that would take them right to Iwo's beaches. Marty was the fifth man back on the right-hand side. In front of him, heads protected by helmets bobbed in time with the ocean. The boats circled in place while US Navy planes zipped overhead, continuing to bomb the island. Streams of smoke curled off the wings of some of the planes, left behind by relentless machine gun fire. Shells released from the bellies of bombers plummeted to the earth.

For two hours, Marty watched the attack from his Higgins boat. He felt removed. The scene looked more like something he'd seen at the movie theater back home.

It was at the movie theater that Marty had first considered joining this war. He was just fifteen years old. On a Sunday in

December, he'd gone to see a film with friends and was heading out to the lobby to get more popcorn when he overheard a few adults talking about something called Pearl Harbor. *What is Pearl Harbor?* he wondered. *What does that mean?*

Word came through to the Higgins boat: it was time to make the run to the beach. They sped up, joining with the other boats that had been circling while waiting for the signal. Overhead, the aircraft continued their assault on the island, focusing heavily on Mount Suribachi, the peak that stood taller than five hundred feet at the base of Iwo Jima.

As the boat raced to shore, Marty looked up at the planes, trying to distract himself by counting the Corsairs and Hellcats, just like he used to count ducks and geese on his hunting trips back home. Hunting calmed him, helped clear his mind; retreating to those thoughts was like a comforting old friend offering shelter. The aircraft kept up their attack even as the boats neared the shore, suppressing any gunfire from the Japanese soldiers waiting to defend the island.

Marty's team was going to land between Red Beach One and Red Beach Two, near the base of Suribachi. As the boat approached the shoreline, someone shouted, "Okay, brace yourself!"

In front of Marty, the ramp dropped, revealing absolute chaos. Bodies littered the sand. Oddly, he saw only Americans; there was not a Japanese soldier in sight. Without time to process what he saw, Marty rushed out of the boat and onto Iwo Jima's shore, the dark sand the color of chimney soot. His feet never touched the water.

Any fantasy he'd possibly harbored about being a Hollywood war hero evaporated in that instant, he'd later tell his oldest son, because chaos raged everywhere he turned.

He ran along the beach to his right, the waterlogged sand providing firm footing. He passed by a depression in the sand, formed by a shell explosion. There were two Marines in the crater. Marty was struck by how young they looked. One was missing a chunk of his arm, thin shreds of skin the only thing keeping the hand connected at the wrist. Both had bled out, their bodies the ashen gray of death. Marty had been on Iwo for less than a minute. He stared at them and thought, *Connor, what the hell are you doing here?*

There wasn't time to dwell on the question. Ahead of him, Marty saw two Marines, "old salts" with decades of combat experience between them. He and his friend Paul Bellows made the snap decision to follow them. Dunes of black sand known as terraces rose steeply on their left, fifteen to twenty feet high. To escape the open beach, where they were easy targets, the small group tried to climb the terraces, sinking immediately to their shins in the soft sand. Marty shimmied up at a crawl, using his rifle for traction. Incoming bullets and mortars were swallowed up by the sand all around them.

After scaling the terraces, the four Marines headed toward one of two active airstrips on Iwo. A dozen damaged Japanese Zeros, the famed enemy fighter planes, were pushed off to the side of the runway like scraps at a junkyard. Marty thought it would be the perfect hiding place for a sniper, so he kept a watchful eye trained on the area.

These airstrips were the reason the Marines were on this island. Controlling Iwo Jima, located just 760 miles from Tokyo, would give the Allies the ability to land massive American B-29 bombers on the island for refueling and emergencies. Without Iwo, the campaign to bomb mainland Japan would be in jeopardy. The Americans sought to gain this crucial advantage; the Japanese desperately needed to defend it. Caught in the middle, thousands of men from both sides would die on a volcanic rock no larger than eight square miles.

As the four Marines approached the airstrip, constant mortar fire and the staccato of machine guns burst through the air. Marty saw men dropping all around him. The relentless gunfire sounded so close. Paul looked at Marty and could tell he was nervous.

"You never hear the one that hits you," Paul assured him.

Marty nodded. Moments later, a loud whoosh filled his ears. Instinct born from endless training took over as Marty and the others tripped themselves by putting one foot behind the other and hitting the deck, throwing their arms out with their weapons in front of them while keeping their faces from ramming into the backs of their rifles.[2] Out of nowhere, a shell came hurtling through the air and exploded right next to them, covering them in charcoal-colored sand. Shrapnel shredded through Marty's pack, but his body was untouched. He lifted his head and looked at Paul.

"You son of a bitch," Marty said, spitting sand. "I thought you said I'd never hear the one that hit me! They don't come any closer."

The thought entered his mind again. *What the hell am I doing here?*

Martin Charles Connor Jr. was born on April 16, 1926, in Syracuse, New York. He shared a name with his father, a second-generation Irish American. His mother, Edna Ostrom Connor, was Swedish Irish. Both were devout Catholics, and they raised their five children as such. Mass on Sunday was not to be missed, and prayers before mealtime and bedtime were a must.

Marty was the second oldest. As a boy, he'd sit with his father in the living room of their home on Strathmore Drive. After dinner, Martin Sr. would light up a cigar and read the paper. If young Marty was lucky, he'd make smoke rings for Marty, who would try to stick his finger in the middle of the wispy circles like hitting a bull's-eye.

A few years after Marty was born, the Great Depression hit, but if the family felt the effects, Martin Sr., an insurance agent and accountant, and Edna, a mother and housewife, kept it from the children. The milkman still came by, his horse-drawn wagon carrying the week's offerings. Coal deliveries also came to the house, during a time before gas heat. The truck would pull up to the driveway and unload into a chute leading to the basement. Marty's father would shovel the coal into the furnace. Together, they'd carry a pail of ashes back upstairs, Marty on one side, his father on the other.

Between chores and church, what Marty craved most was the outdoors. While his brother played sports like basketball and baseball, and two of his three sisters were cheerleaders, Marty wasn't interested. For him, it was all about hunting.

Pheasants ran wild by the wooded area near their house, which sat on Syracuse's city limits. His springer spaniel by his side, Marty would hunt with friends and fish the streams; a can of worms as bait and a sandwich for lunch could last him all day. By the age of sixteen, he'd shot his first deer. He counted down the school days until Saturday arrived and he could be outside once more, hunting with his gun. It was a skill that would serve him well.

Night blanketed Iwo in a heavy darkness. Marty had survived the first day, but he was in no mood to sleep. He and what was left of his battalion had traveled west and a bit back toward Mount Suribachi, digging in for the night in its shadow. A piece of advice spread through the ranks: don't look up. Naval ships offshore were still firing on the island, lighting up the night sky. Those shell fragments had to land somewhere.

From his foxhole, Marty saw a road branching out from the north. This would be the perfect place for a tank attack, he thought. Yet all he had to defend himself were two grenades and, having ditched his rifle in the earlier chaos, a short-barreled shotgun gritty with sand. He unhooked his grenades and put them on a little shelf he had dug into the foxhole wall. Just as with the landing, when he had placed tape over the pins, he wasn't taking any chances. Others were not so careful, and the occasional sound of grenade explosions pierced the night.

Sleep would not come.

Neither did hunger. Two other Marines, including a Texan named Charles Hale, crouched in the foxhole with Marty. The others ate their D-Day rations, which included a special fruit-and-nut bar made in Hawaii. Marty left his food untouched.

The next morning, the adrenaline finally wore off long enough to trigger hunger. Marty opened his rations, figuring he'd start with the fruit bar. When he unwrapped it, it appeared to be alive, wriggling and white, covered in maggots.

There were stories. They all knew them. Marty heard guys say the "Japs" would burn cigarettes in prisoners' eyes. *Don't get taken prisoner, and take no prisoners.* In many ways, the traditional rules of war did not apply in the Pacific.

They knew that at Japanese prisoner-of-war (POW) camps, American soldiers, sailors, airmen, and Marines were tortured by the Japanese to the brink of death and beyond. The Marines were taught that the Japanese were "lousy, sneaky, treacherous," and to stay on guard at all times.[3]

The ingrained hatred had begun long before a Japanese Zero pilot ever had a battleship deck at Pearl Harbor in his crosshairs. In the United States, certain phrases, nicknames, and news stories used derogatory labels not just for Japanese people but for anyone of Asian descent within America's borders. As early as 1905, the *San Francisco Chronicle*, one of the most influential newspapers on the West Coast, featured a nine-column spread on February 23. The headline, splashed across the front page directly under the masthead, declared, "Japanese Invasion, the Problem of the Hour for United States."[4] Despite the militarized implications of "invasion," the story had nothing to do with war and instead had everything to do with immigration, containing hardly veiled references to the threat of "little brown men" to "white man's work"—an issue "pressing upon California and upon the entire United States as heavily and contains as much of a menace as the matter of Chinese immigration ever did."

It was only the beginning. The *Chronicle* continued its push, ending any pretense of labor concerns and leaning into "blatant fearmongering," with headlines including "Brown Men an Evil in the Public Schools" (March 5, 1905) and repeated references to Japanese and Chinese people as "the yellow peril."[5]

Other newspapers featured cartoons with caricatures of Japanese people, turning them into animals like rabid dogs, rats, monkeys, lice, or other insects.[6] Restaurants boasted that they poisoned "rats and Japs"; barbershops offered free shaves for Japanese with the threat of "accidents" for a slipped blade along the neck.[7] Kids knew the worst insult you could level at someone was to call them a "dirty Jap rat."[8]

The propaganda machine churned and churned, effectively painting all Japanese people as a "subhuman race," feeding on an overall "long-festered" anti-Asian sentiment that "bubbled to the surface and fueled the fury of millions."[9]

Against this backdrop, President Franklin D. Roosevelt put Executive Order 9066 into effect on February 19, 1942, two months after Pearl Harbor. The word "Japanese" was not present, yet it left no doubt. Under the guise of the order, more than 120,000 people of Japanese descent were confined to internment camps across the western United States within the next six months.[10]

More than half of them were American citizens.

Almost three weeks into the fighting on Iwo Jima, and the dead and dying were all around them. At night, the wind carried the smell of death. It oddly reminded Marty of pancakes on a griddle.

Marty's buddy Charles Hale was a young sharecropper from Texas with an accent to match. He and Marty, who always called Hale by his last name, were in the same tent back at camp and in the same foxhole the first night, and now they huddled together again. When the moon showed itself, Marty would pull his prayer book from his pocket and read. It took his mind off the shelling, at least for a little bit. Hale sometimes asked to see it and prayed too.

Around the twentieth night, Hale, Marty, and another Marine named Jack Gill were in the hole. Jack was a fine fighter. He had already been shot in the shoulder, leaving ranks for barely a day to get bandaged up before rejoining his brothers. In the foxhole, they knew the Japanese were hiding in a complex network of underground tunnels, perhaps even under their own feet. The tunnels layered and sprawled over a total length of eleven miles on the small island.[11]

This was the reason Marty hadn't seen any Japanese soldiers when the Marines landed on the beach three weeks before. In fact, they'd barely seen any since—at least not any live ones. The Japanese had spent months preparing to defend the island. In certain foxholes, Marines could actually hear the Japanese speaking beneath them. It was unnerving; every shadow made the Marines jump.

In front of Marty, Jack, and Hale, a slit showed itself through a depression in the ground, and they could faintly see something, or someone, moving. All three men fired at the same time, killing whoever it was. Marty figured their bullets went straight through the earth. But the shooting had also given away their position. An unseen enemy from a cave nearby began firing into the foxhole in retaliation.

A bullet hissed by Marty's ear, catching Hale in the chest and exiting through his shoulder. Marty dropped down to attend to his friend. "Where did they get you?" he asked. "Where are you hit?"

"It went plumb through," Hale said. Marty saw the gaping hole, felt Hale's blood on his hands. He tried to apply a battle dressing to stop the bleeding. There was so much blood. Too much.

Jack folded his tall frame down next to Marty. "I don't want to be a son of a bitch about this, Marty," he said. "But your buddy's gone."

Hale died in Marty's arms, in that foxhole, under sniper fire from a Japanese soldier they never saw. Marty felt sorry for his friend, for his family in Texas, for being unable to save him. Though Marty was just a teenager himself, he felt protective of Hale. He had failed to shield him. And deep down, Marty felt another type of guilt too.

He was relieved the bullet had missed him.

He and Jack lifted Hale's body from the foxhole, dragging him some twenty feet behind the hole, laying him in a little hollow where the ground was a bit deeper.

He lay there for several days before someone came around to collect the dead.

Postmarked: April 25, 1945
Date on letter: March 24
Addressed to Marty's brother Joe at Strathmore Drive, Syracuse, New York

---

Dear Joe,
As I write this letter I sit in my fox hole, a few hundred yds. from the front lines. I am back here resting up, after six days on the line without sleep and very little food. You don't miss the food up there though, because you don't have any appetite. I have lost a lot of weight on this island. I bet you even weigh more than I do.

We went back and used the Army's showers to-day. First one in thirty days for me. I guess you can call me bathless Connor, from now on.

You wanted me to tell you how it was and still is, in your last letter. I don't like to think about it at all but I will say it's no joke. Last day on the line a sniper shot a buddie of mine who was right next to me in the same fox hole.

I have seen quite a number of nips and some of those I sent to where they can't kill any more Marines and some down near [?] sent me to where I couldn't bother them again either.

To keep our wits about us we were given little containers of 100% proof brandy. It certainly helped a lot, when you were laying in your fox hole, with the rain beating down on you. I'll close for now, be good.

Love your brother,
"Bud"
P.S. Excuse the English and spelling.

Marty had begged his parents to let him join the war. But he was underage and undersized. The scrawny fifteen-year-old, barely five foot eight, who first learned of the war at the Elmwood movie theater on Syracuse's south side, bided his time until he was seventeen, at the height of a young man's most formative years, and then took matters into his own hands.

In October 1943, Marty enlisted in the Marines, the military branch whose values he felt closely mirrored his own—loyalty, honesty, integrity, respect—the same values preached in the house on Strathmore and in the Catholic church every Sunday.

The letter was dated October 11, 1943, on United States Marine Corps letterhead, with the eagle, globe, and anchor emblem in the upper left corner. It had come from the Eastern Recruiting Division Headquarters, Syracuse District, from Room 317 of the New Post Office Building. It was addressed to Martin Charles Conner Jr., his last name misspelled with an *e* instead of the second *o*, at his family's home on Strathmore Drive. And it instructed him to report to that office in two days, on Thursday, October 13, at 9:30 in the morning sharp, to be sworn in to the Marine Corps.

It was signed by a first sergeant, H. T. Murphy.

And it would change the course of Marty's life forever.

Marty reported to boot camp at Parris Island in South Carolina, the first of many stops on a journey that would eventually lead to the Pacific. From there, he went to Camp Lejeune in North Carolina for training, then on a troop train across the country to Camp Pendleton in California. It was there, in January 1944, that the Fifth Marine Division was formed, three months before Marty's eighteenth birthday.

The Fifth Division, eager for combat, participated in training exercises off the coast of California. Eventually, the call came through. Maneuvers for that day ended early, and the Marines were told they'd be shipping out overseas. Marty boarded a ship headed for Guam. For two weeks, they floated near the island as offshore reserve. But their number was never called. Disappointed, Marty and the rest of the division set sail for Hawaii for more training.

Camp Tarawa was in the middle of Hawaii's Big Island, framed by a resort-dotted coast on one side and sugarcane fields on the other. Again they trained, practicing landings in the

Higgins boats and scaling cargo nets on the ships. Feet in the horizontal, hands in the vertical. Over and over and over again, they worked until it became as automatic as tying their combat boots. Still, the Marines were anxious. A world war was on, and they remained on the sidelines.

That was about to change. In January 1945, a year after the division was formed, the Fifth Marines got the call. Marty boarded the USS *Deuel*, part of a convoy that would number some eight hundred ships, all headed for an unknown destination in the Pacific.

This time, they would not be offshore reserve. Two days into the journey, the secret destination previously referred to only as "Island X" became a volcanic rock called Iwo Jima.

Marty Connor,
Camp Lejeune, 1943
(courtesy Connor family)

Postmarked: March 10, 1945
Date on letter: Feb. 24, 1945
Addressed to Marty's parents

Dear Folks,

I am fine and still kicking. I suppose you know, that I am fighting on <u>Iwojima</u>. *Our outfit is doing a swell job here. I know now what Sherman meant when he said war is hell. This has been hell from the very first. I can't say very much about the way things are, or our losses. The nips here are not like I pictured them. They are good sized men. They only gave me one sheet of v mail, so I am not able to write to Mary Lou. Call her up Mom, and tell her I said hello. She is a swell girl, she writes to me every day. So long for now. Pray for me—Love Bud*

Postmarked: March 9, 1945
Date on letter: Feb. 1945

Dear Mom + Dad,

At this moment I am in my fox hole. It is about five foot deep, five foot long, and two foot wide. I can hear the shells going over head toward the Jap lines. Also the Jap shells coming my way. I received holy communion the other night from our chaplain and also three times aboard ship. I have been a good boy, so I am not <u>too</u> worried over the outcome of this campaign. If God wants to take me, I shall be ready, although I pray constantly not to get hit. Well I'll say so long for now. Be good, say a few prayers for me.

Love Bud

The fighting was slow, and at close range. There were few places to take cover on the barren volcanic island, devoid of grass or much greenery at all, "like a piece of the moon that had dropped down to earth."[12]

Day after day, the action remained largely the same: fire a barrage of artillery in the morning, get the order to move out, climb out of the foxholes with all the gear, and advance as far as they could.

The Japanese quickly caught on. When the artillery stopped coming from the Americans, they knew the advance was close behind. The Japanese soldiers emerged from caves and tunnels, taking up veiled positions to gun down the Marines like a deadly welcome party. Some days, Marty's battalion would advance two hundred yards; other days, only twenty feet.

The weather didn't help. Unlike many other islands of the Pacific, which were covered in jungle, Iwo was desolate and windy. It was March, and at night the temperature dipped. Driving rain sent Marines scrambling under ponchos, desperate to keep their weapons dry.

One night, soaked to the bone, Marty couldn't stop shaking. He emerged from his foxhole to find a discarded backpack. He wasn't sure if the owner was wounded or killed, but he was too cold to care. He rifled through the pack in the dark, his hands finding something that felt like wool. It was a thick shirt. Marty put it on, immediately feeling warmer. He found a pair of pants too. Marty pried off his boots and peeled his wet uniform away from his legs. His pants were soaked through, as if he'd gone swimming in them. He put on the dry pants from the pack and some fresh socks.

By the time he slid back into the foxhole, he "felt alive again."

Sleepless night after sleepless night, Marty tried to picture himself walking off Iwo Jima. But he never could. It seemed impossible. There were too many close calls.

Perhaps the closest came one night around midnight. Marty and another Marine were relieved by two others who'd come to man the mortar at their position. Marty lay down behind the gun and fell asleep in the foxhole. The next thing he remembered was a voice he recognized hollering, "Who goes there?"

"Is that you, Fred?" Marty replied. He walked toward the voice, only then realizing where he was. Marty had sleepwalked out of the foxhole, in between the American front and the Japanese line, into no-man's land. A Marine named Fred Beymer, whom Marty hadn't seen in more than a year, called out to him, requiring name and unit. When Marty made it over to him, Fred told him he'd challenged Marty three times. "That was the last time I was going to challenge you," Fred added. "I was going to open up with the machine gun here!"

"Fred, I only heard you the one time," Marty said. Another moment longer, and Fred likely would have pulled the trigger. More than ever, Marty was convinced that his survival was the work of a guardian angel. How else could he explain wandering through no-man's land without getting shot, and then recognizing the voice that challenged him?

"Jesus saved me," he said to Fred. Marty did not doubt it.

Postmarked: March 21, 1945
Date on letter: March 8, 1945

Dear Folks, I just got back from the front lines this morning.
Last night myself and another fellow operated a 60 M.M.

*mortar for about six hours, then we got a relief. We jumped
into a foxhole and fell asleep. A while later, I started walking in
my sleep. I got out of my foxhole and started walking towards
the Jap lines. A buddie of mine with a Thomson sub-machine
gun halted me. If he hadn't recognized me he would have let
me have it. I have to sign off now folks. Be good. Pray for me.
Love Bud*

Postmarked: March 21, 1945
Date on letter: March 9, 1945

---

*Dear Mom + Dad,
We just had a mail call, I got eleven letters, I don't want
you folks at home to worry about me. I think everything will
be alright. I have lived through the worst that the nips have
thrown at us. I haven't got that shot-gun any more. It got
all shot up in an artillery barrage. I dropped it at the top of
my fox hole, as I heard the nips shells whistling in. I lost five of
my best buddies in that barrage. I have been very lucky all the
way through, I know God is with me and watching over me.
Dave Osborn got it in the back by a sniper. I think he will be
all right. So long for now. Pray for me. Love Bud*

At one point on Iwo, Marty came up behind a Japanese soldier in a spider hole—a one-man, camouflaged foxhole. The soldier was alive but no longer a threat. He seemed out of his mind.
Too many concussions, Marty figured.

He found some telephone wire and looped it under the soldier's arms to lift him from the hole. He had to be careful in case
it was a trap, in case the soldier was sitting on a charge ready

to detonate without his weight on it. Marty turned around to get some help when another Marine walked up to them with a machine gun. With Marty still kneeling next to the dazed, defenseless soldier, the other Marine pumped him full of bullets and walked away.

It was a moment that would stick with Marty forever, symbolic of the visceral hate of wartime that clouded better judgment.

In *Looking for the Good War*, Elizabeth D. Samet wrote about a naval officer on Guam named Robert Fitzgerald who highlighted the "particular brutality" of the Pacific Theater, "where the violence was admixed with and intensified by racial animosity, which expressed itself in mutilation and the taking of trophies and reached its apogee in the firebombing of scores of Japanese cities and the dropping of atomic bombs on Hiroshima and Nagasaki."[13]

The taking of those trophies—the flags, diaries, photos, swords—ran rampant through the ranks. On Guadalcanal, in September 1942, there existed a "thriving black market in Japanese souvenirs" among the Marines.[14] On New Georgia, part of the Solomon Islands, which saw a fierce battle for control of the Munda Point airfield in July and August 1943, souvenir hunters wasted no time "stripping" disabled Japanese aircraft, including Zeros and bombers.[15] Even news correspondents would occasionally pocket what they found.[16]

There was an element of "savagery" in the Pacific that was not found in Europe, observed US Marine E. B. Sledge. On the island of Peleliu in the fall of 1944, during any lull in the fighting, "the men stripped the packs and pockets of the enemy dead for souvenirs," Sledge wrote in *With the Old Breed*, calling it a "gruesome business" but one the Marines handled "in a most methodical manner." He noted the helmets checked for tiny flags, the emptying of knapsacks and uniform pockets. "Highly prized" items included swords, handguns, and hara-kiri knives, snatched to become personal mementos or even "sold to some pilot or sailor for a fat price," implying the desire for souvenirs even among those who most likely would never come face to face with the enemy.[17]

"The men gloated over, compared, and often swapped their prizes," Sledge wrote. "It was uncivilized, as is all war, and was carried out with that particular savagery that characterized the struggle between the Marines and the Japanese. It wasn't simply souvenir hunting or looting the enemy dead; it was more like Indian warriors taking scalps."

He watched as a man he knew "removed a Nambu pistol, slipped the belt off the corpse, and took the leather holster. He pulled off the steel helmet, reached inside, and took out a neatly folded Japanese flag covered with writing. The veteran pitched the helmet on the coral where it clanked and rattled, rolled the corpse over, and started pawing through the combat pack. The veteran's buddy came up and started stripping the other Japanese corpses."

The young Sledge was horrified, unable to even move or speak, "just glued to the spot almost in a trance." The looted corpses were "sprawled" around him, the other Marine and his buddy having moved on to new priorities. Sledge's mind raced.

"Would I become this casual and calloused about enemy dead?" he remembered wondering in the moment. "Would the war dehumanize me so that I, too, could 'field strip' enemy dead with such nonchalance?"

The answer was yes: "The time soon came when it didn't bother me a bit."

Of course, like most things in war, and in human nature, it was not cut-and-dried. Not all the GIs were racist; not all racists took souvenirs. (Though, as Ernie Pyle wrote during Okinawa in April 1945, "all Marines are souvenir hunters.")[18] After all, the practice of trophy taking has existed since wars themselves. But during the Second World War, there seemed to have been a particular Americanism attached to the custom. Having just emerged from the Great Depression, gripped by a sense of materialism, of ownership, of opportunity, American GIs across Europe, Africa, and Asia seemed to take all they could carry.

Although the seizing of wartime trophies appeared to reach a "mania" during both world wars, Samet observed that perhaps it was connected to something more than materialism at best, or racism at worst.[19] In *The Warriors: Reflections on Men in Battle*, US Army veteran J. Glenn Gray wrote that the desire for souvenirs was not merely to prove that the soldier had been there, or even from "a primitive desire to loot," but rather for "some assurance of his future beyond the destructive environment of the present."[20]

Yet when American GIs held up the Japanese battle flags they took as trophies, posing for photographs, what would they have thought if they could have read the inscriptions? Would they have thought of their own families, their mothers and fathers and sisters and brothers, their girlfriends and wives and aunts and uncles?

In the heat of the moment, it likely wouldn't have mattered much; the bloody battlefields of the Pacific arena operated in a system of kill or be killed, and race-driven hatred ran bone deep on both sides. But one wonders what it might have meant if those Japanese characters did not reinforce the concept of foreign, of other, but instead were English letters and words that US soldiers, sailors, and Marines could read.

Marty Connor survived thirty-six days on Iwo Jima, the full length of the campaign. It would become the Marines' bloodiest battle of World War II. The Marines suffered around twenty-eight thousand casualties, including some sixty-eight hundred dead. Of the estimated twenty-one thousand Japanese fighters marooned on the island, less than a thousand survived.

On the transport ship back to Hawaii, the once-filled mess hall had cleared out. On the way to Iwo, the Marines had had to stand and eat shoulder to shoulder; now there were plenty of open seats. When Marty had landed on Iwo, the skinny kid from Syracuse had weighed around 150 pounds; just over a month later, he barely tipped the scale at 120.

Back at camp, Marty walked into the tent he'd once shared with Hale and the others. The 1st Battalion, Marty's battalion, had more enlisted men killed in action than any other from the 26th Regiment.[21] Of the eight bunks, only two were filled, Marty's included. The others would remain empty until a fresh crop of young recruits was sent to fill them.

Marty might have been leaving Iwo Jima behind, but he did not leave empty-handed. When he had returned to the transport ship, he needed a hand to hoist himself back on board. Two sailors lifted Marty over the rail and onto the deck. He lay there on his back, looking up at the sky, happy to be alive.

The sailors had to help Marty not only because he was weak; he was also weighted down. Not immune to the practice of souvenir hunting, Marty had carefully tucked away in his pack the trophies he'd taken from the battlefield. He had photos, letters, pay records, a diary, a white shirt, Japanese grenades and knives and guns; at one point, he had a bloodstained helmet clipped to his pack, but someone had stolen it from him. Back on the ship, to make sure no one would take anything else, he stashed his mementos out of sight, hidden under a blanket in his bunk.

Marty couldn't read the letters or the diary—they were written in Japanese. He didn't know the faces in the photographs—they were family members of the dead soldiers. But he took those items, as so many others did. Pieces of the war were going home with him, though he'd need no reminders. Instead, those pieces would fade into the background of Marty's life for several decades, before returning to the forefront with a new purpose. A higher purpose, perhaps, for a young kid from Syracuse who, despite Iwo's nearly fifty thousand casualties, somehow managed to walk off the island with barely a scratch.

Postmarked: April 30, 1945
Date on letter: April 27, 1945

Dear Folks,

Here I am again, anything new back home? . . .

I just got through reading a letter I received on Iwo, from you. You all seemed very worried about me at the time.

If I am going to get killed, I'll get killed, there is no use in your worrying. I wasn't afraid of dying on Iwo. I was a good boy and I know I wouldn't go to hell if I died. I think of dying as being something wonderful, and when my time does come, you can bet your boots I'll be ready.

Marty Connor (fifth from the right in the back row) and
fellow Marines on Iwo Jima, posing with their war trophies,
March 24, 1945 (courtesy Connor family)

CHAPTER 4

OKINAWA AND MAINLAND JAPAN / 1945

On April 1, less than a week after suffering a devastating loss at Iwo Jima, Japan came under attack once again. Like hopping rock by rock across a river, the Americans were taking island after island, getting ever closer to mainland Japan. On Easter Sunday, more than 180,000 US troops descended on Okinawa in a final push toward Tokyo. Japanese troops numbering 130,000 waited for them, holding fire until they had the Americans pinned in the teeth of the island's rugged subtropical landscape.

Among the Japanese troops was Masamitsu Shiokawa. Only eight months before, in the midst of the raging war, the thirty-year-old and his wife, Kimiko, had welcomed a baby boy in the hospital of Yawata Steel Works, where Masamitsu worked each day. They named him Masataka (正隆), one letter from each of the names of his father's two younger brothers: Kiyotaka (清隆) and Masayoshi (正喜).

"It seems like my father was going back to the war to die," Masataka wrote in his 2015 memoir.[1] When Masamitsu was called up to rejoin the military service ahead of Okinawa, Kimiko said she would go to the Yasukuni Shrine, believed to house the souls of those lost while defending Japan, to pray for her husband if the worst should happen. "I am not going to the Yasukuni," Masamitsu replied. "I am not going to die."

Yet Masataka feels that his namesakes, Masamitsu's two younger brothers, were chosen to "take care of [Masamitsu's] fatherless son," even though Masamitsu planned to defy a nearly inevitable demise. "I am not going to die" were the last words Masamitsu spoke to his wife.

A week after Masataka was born, Masamitsu received orders to join the war effort in Okinawa. He was assigned to the 116th Platoon, 36th Regiment; it was a communications unit, not a combat one, and his wife prayed it meant he'd be spared from the front lines.

Masamitsu Shiokawa (courtesy Masataka Shiokawa)

Postcards from the island soon began arriving at home. Although Masamitsu, who had previous experience censoring military correspondence, was careful not to divulge any sensitive information, he still gave advice to his family from the field as he and thousands of other Japanese troops prepared for an inevitable American invasion. In his fourth postcard, he recommended that his young wife and newborn son evacuate Yawata-shi, where they'd been living near the steelworks, which had already seen air raids by American forces. First, of course, Masamitsu asked about his son.

"Is Masataka doing well?" he wrote. "Do not worry about me. As for the house, how about (evacuating) since there is no business with the Yawata Steel Works any more. If it is too hard for you to do that, then I will not force you. But I think you should move to Saga [prefecture] with your mother."

Kimiko heeded the advice. Because of that, Masataka writes, he was able to "spend the next 70 years safely."

The tenth postcard was postmarked November 17, 1944. "I am relieved you have evacuated," Masamitsu wrote to his wife. He asked her to write to his parents from time to time. All four of their sons had been conscripted into the war. "I have received your postcard too," he continued. "Thank you. Because [Saga prefecture] has more food and better air, Masataka will grow well. If there is no father around, the child will end up being too spoiled, so be careful."

These postcards, it seemed, were a lifeline for Masamitsu. Stationed in Naha, today the capital city of Okinawa, he and his fellow soldiers were subject to frequent air raids. "Sleepless night with all the memories," Masamitsu wrote in a poem he included in a postcard. "My home comes to mind in spite of myself."

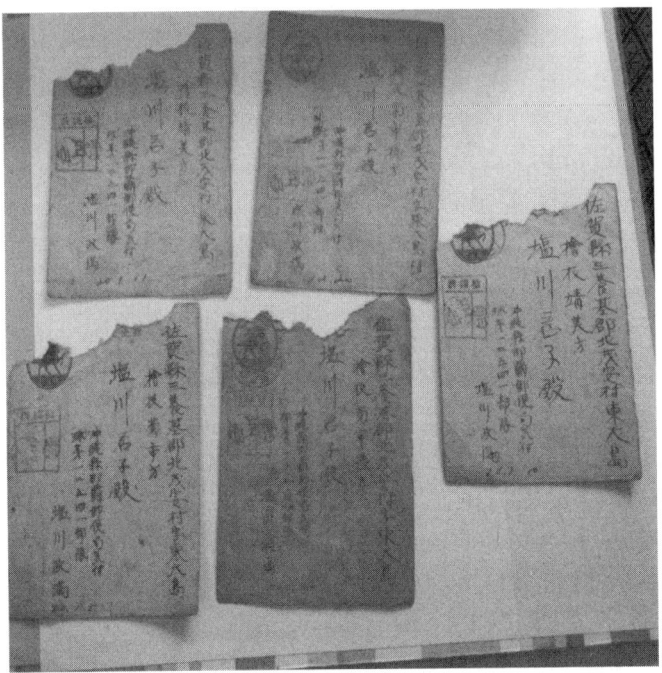

A selection of postcards sent home by Masamitsu Shiokawa
during the war (courtesy Masataka Shiokawa)

The eleventh postcard was dated November 18. "It has been cooler here," Masamitsu wrote. "Please feel relieved to know that I am doing and working well. How is Masataka? I am sure he is doing great, but I want to have a look."

Those last six words would eventually consume much of his son's life. "Each time I read his words, 'I want to have a look,'" Masataka later wrote, "I am so moved by his eager feelings and I cannot stop crying."

The postcards from Masamitsu kept coming, roughly thirty in all and each asking about his son, until one day they didn't. His last was dated February 3, 1945—just two weeks before Marty

Connor and the US Marines landed on Iwo Jima. "How is Masa-taka?" he faithfully wrote. "I am worrying about him because it is cold there. I started home remittance from January. I arranged to send 85 yen. Please let me know when you receive it. Please be careful not to catch cold and not let him catch cold."

After that, communications were cut off. Following their bloody victory on Iwo Jima, the Americans were coming closer and closer to Okinawa, and therefore mainland Japan. Japanese forces prepared their troops to do whatever was necessary to prevent an invasion.

What Masamitsu would have experienced on Okinawa was among the worst in a Pacific War filled with worsts. If he had dared catch a glimpse of the waters off the island on the first day of April, he would have seen more ships and troops preparing for invasion than in any other battle in the region, second only to D-Day at Normandy, which was the largest amphibious invasion in history. More than thirteen hundred American ships, along with fifty British ships, ferried four divisions from the US Army and two from the Marine Corps—more than half a million soldiers and Marines.[2]

Waiting for the Americans, not on the beaches but firmly entrenched in Okinawa's interior—a subtropical jungle landscape—were over one hundred thousand Japanese soldiers and civilians, who had been forced into conscription by the imperial forces after Japan claimed ownership of the island in 1879. Once independent, with different cultural traditions and heritage, Okinawa became part of Japan but was treated "little better than a colony and a neglected one at that."[3]

The Japanese forces, the bulk of whom were made up by the Imperial 32nd Army, led by Lieutenant General Mitsuru Ushijima, waited and waited as the Americans advanced into the heart of their defense.[4] In a feat of backbreaking work, tens of thousands of Japanese soldiers, conscripted civilians, and forced Korean laborers had constructed another extensive network of tunnels and caves.[5] In the planning stages, the Americans referred to their plans for Okinawa as Operation Iceberg.[6] The Okinawans called it "tetsu no ame"—typhoon of steel.[7]

Torrential rains and endless bloodshed created boot-sucking mud. Bombardments poured from the sky in quantities that rivaled the rain. The terrain was unforgiving. Food supplies were insufficient. The caves were suffocating, unyielding, lacking fresh air or water. It sounded above as if the very world was ending—with American naval firepower that "shook the earth"— before the personal combat even began.[8]

And the knowledge that Okinawa was the Allies' last step before reaching mainland Japan created an intense desperation among the men on the island, fueled by hatred and fear.

Japan's propaganda machine had been as active as America's before and during the war, rooted in a deep sense of nationalism that had begun with the Meiji Restoration in 1868.[9] It was a new national identity that became "more enmeshed with the psychological preparation for war." By 1890, the Imperial Rescript on Education was a "sacred text," requiring Japan's citizens to swear "loyalty and filial piety to the emperor and [to pledge], should they be required, to sacrifice their lives in his name." It was required memorization for all students—a way of life "rooted in Emperor worship and a caste system based on strict submission."[10]

By the 1930s, according to renowned historian John W. Dower, much of Japan's propaganda drummed up fear around the rise of communism in China, "fixated not merely on the 'White Peril' of European and American imperialism, but also on the 'Red Peril' of Soviet-led international communism."[11] In schools, students were taught the phrase "Kichiku Beiei"— "Americans and British are devils."[12]

Yet as Japan's defenses fell to Allied forces, island after island, one after the next and ever closer to Okinawa, the propaganda machine worked double-time. Much as in the US, caricatures, including cartoons of "apelike Americans," permeated popular culture.[13] Both in and out of schools, Japanese and Okinawan civilians were taught to fear racist Americans, who were poised to "rule the world and to torture, rape, murder, or enslave all Asians."

The fear was so deeply instilled that during the battle, civilians in Okinawa were seen throwing themselves, and even their children, off cliff faces into the turquoise waters rather than risk capture. Others refused to leave their hiding places in natural caves across the island, often ending up sealed inside.[14]

The battle raged on, and one month became two, then three. Japanese forces, with their conscripted Okinawan civilians, suffered incredible losses against superior American airpower and US troops, who faced mounting casualties of their own from repeated kamikaze attacks and close-range, hand-to-hand fighting.[15]

Hills bearing names such as Sugar Loaf and Half Moon would enter battlefield lore. The dead piled up. Wounded Japanese had few options but to rely on each other, their medical capabilities gravely depleted. Caves were designated as hospital areas, yet "crowding was terrible, fleas abundant, and medical facilities rudimentary," proving little better than the battlefield itself.[16]

Out of desperation, an official Imperial Army strategy was to deploy soldiers to "conduct guerrilla warfare" in central and northern areas of the island. Others entrenched themselves deeper into the land, using the ridges and terrain to their advantage.[17]

"It was the most ghastly corner of hell I had ever witnessed," US Marine E. B. Sledge would later write in *With the Old Breed*. "As far as I could see, an area that previously had been a low grassy valley with a picturesque stream meandering through it was a muddy, repulsive, open sore on the land. The place was choked with the putrefaction of death, decay, and destruction."[18]

In the midst of the brutality, souvenir hunting continued. In addition to the usual trophies—the flags and personal effects—another coveted category seemed to increase in popularity as the fighting in the Pacific went on, hitting a crescendo on Okinawa: gold teeth.

There were several methods for extraction, but the most common seemed to be with the Marine-issued KA-BAR knife. The blade's tip went onto the tooth of the Japanese soldier—who was usually dead, but by at least one witness's account, not always—and the hilt of the knife was struck with force, knocking the tooth free.

"One of my buddies carried a bunch of 'em in a sock," Sledge told Studs Terkel for Terkel's 1984 oral history of the war. "How could American boys do this?" Sledge continued. "If you're reduced to savagery by a situation, anything's possible. When Lindbergh made a trip to the Philippines, he was horrified at the way the American GIs talked about the Japanese. It was so savage. We *were* savages."[19]

Masamitsu Shiokawa was killed during the battle. He left behind his wife, Kimiko, and his ten-month-old son, Masataka. Quoting Masamitsu's military record, his son later wrote, "'On June 22, Showa 20 [1945], Komesu on Okinawa main island, died in a battle.' There are no feelings in these words, just a few words."

The timing proved devastating. That same day, the commanders in charge of Japan's defense of the island died by suicide, effectively ending the fight in Okinawa, which, along with military casualties, had taken the lives of an estimated 150,000 civilian noncombatants, leaving a traumatic and complicated legacy that reverberates to this day.[20]

Afterward, a small box showed up at the Shiokawa household. It came from the Japanese government, and it had some writing on it: "Soul stone from Okinawa." Inside lay five pieces of stone and coral. They were supposed to represent Masamitsu's remains.

This was the only thing the family would ever receive for his sacrifice.

On August 6, 1945, a day before Masataka Shiokawa's first birthday, the United States dropped an atomic bomb on Hiroshima, and another one three days later on Nagasaki. The war had come to a devastating and unthinkable end. It was in this climate that Masataka grew up, in a Japan occupied by the enemy, the ones who had killed his father.

Family life was difficult. Many of the elder Shiokawa men had been killed in the war. In rural Japan, Masataka and his mother scraped by as amateur farmers. A small rice paddy near their village had a communal irrigation pump. It was precious, and a target for thieves. To protect it, the village residents decided that farmers would take turns watching over it at night. That included Masataka's mother. As she huddled in the pump shack, her young son was home alone, terrified. Some nights, he was so scared that he ran a third of a mile by himself, tears streaming down his face, just to be with her.

There were happier moments, too, and for Masataka they often involved baseball with friends from the neighborhood. Their makeshift baseball field was a rice paddy after harvest, though they were often chased away by the farmer. The boys made do with a stick for a bat, and they fashioned a ball from old pieces of cloth rolled together as firmly as possible. When they'd play during lunch breaks at school, without gloves, the ball would sting their bare hands in the cold of winter.

Masataka knew how hard his mother worked to provide for their little family of two. Besides farming, she took up sewing

A young Masataka Shiokawa and his mother (courtesy Masataka Shiokawa)

and sometimes worked as a cosmetics saleswoman. Masataka attended high school on scholarship (even with his father's war pension, they could not afford school for him) and then university. He worked part-time jobs and later earned a full-time salary, and he always gave every bit of his earnings to his mother. Until he got married at age twenty-three, he'd never even opened one of his paychecks.

Life for Masataka and his mother was quiet. He cherished his mother, but the young boy yearned for more family, to be surrounded by relatives. Occasionally he'd visit his grandparents, aunt and uncle, and cousins. When he returned home, he felt the crushing loneliness of life without his father. Spending time with other family members seemed to make the loss all the more apparent.

He once worked up the courage to tell his mother how he felt. "It's alright," she replied, "you have me." She reminded him of an orphan in a nearby village who'd lost both his parents in the war. She was trying to console her son by offering some perspective, but her remark only worsened his guilt.

Outwardly, Masataka shielded his loneliness. On the inside, it was unbearable.

CHAPTER 5

The train shuddered to a stop. Marty Connor stepped onto the platform. It was after eleven thirty at night, and he could feel the chilled air of his home city through his olive wool uniform. He looked forward to a hot meal that was anything but corned beef; the military must have been trying to get rid of its supplies, because it seemed as if the Marines ate corned beef twice a day every day on the voyage home.[1]

He shouldered his bag and headed for the taxi stand, instructing the driver to drop him off at the end of Strathmore Drive; he wanted to walk home, to savor the moment. On Iwo Jima, he had been unable to picture himself ever walking down this street again. A year had passed since the end of the battle, since Marty's regiment had suffered more casualties than any of the others. A year since he'd left the island physically—but not mentally. Perhaps he never would.

He carried Iwo Jima with him wherever he went, even as the atomic bombs plunged from the sky and war ended in the Pacific. In the months following Japan's surrender, US troops, including Marty, became occupational forces.

The assignment would bring him face to face with the enemy in a completely different context.

The previous September, six months removed from Iwo Jima and just a month after the atomic bombings, Marty and members of the Fifth Marine Division had been sent to Sasebo, Japan, part of Nagasaki prefecture on Kyushu island, along Japan's southwestern coast.[2] In a letter sent home to his parents, postmarked with an airmail stamp that cost six cents, Marty detailed his life as part of the American occupation.[3]

On the day of arrival, reveille on ship was at three in the morning, followed by food and a shower, and then a final check of his gear (which included grenades, ammunition for mortars, and his rifle)—similar to the prelanding processes he'd followed ahead of Iwo Jima. At eight a.m., the Marines landed in the rain. They marched some eight miles to an area with docks and lice-filled warehouses, where Marty and two others stood guard, on duty to protect two steel mills and a woodshop.

By September 23, they had moved out again, only to spend the next day and night at a railroad station before setting up in a former Japanese boot camp. It was "twice as good as Parris Island," Marty told his parents, though it needed a serious deep cleaning and treatment with insecticide. There were plans to establish a hospital, Marty wrote, and while he reiterated on paper, for seemingly the hundredth time, that he did not want them to worry, his battalion doctor suggested sending him there for a run of penicillin to help treat his ear. "I didn't tell you before," he wrote, "but on Iwo I got a ruptured ear drum from concussion and the reason it hasn't healed is because of an acute mastoid that is draining through a hole in the ear drum."

Along with the updates on his whereabouts and his ailing ear, he told his parents about another experience, one that demonstrated a dissonance between curiosity and prejudice that was common at the time.

"We have some Japs working for us," Marty wrote. "Last night I ran into three or four of them fixing some lights, so I thought I'd try my Jap dialect on them. I asked them for a light bulb in Jap and one of them, an officer, knew English, so he started shooting the breeze with me. He asked me a lot of questions, one of them was how old I was."

In the middle of this story, he paused to write, "We sleep four men to a room. So you can see we are not over crowded at all." He also wrote, "When a Jap woman sees you she bows down to you and a Jap man gives you a salute. They are a very dirty race of people. I wouldn't ever want to touch one of them."

Less than a week later, Marty penned another letter to his mother and father, this time on a piece of American Red Cross stationery, from an outpost where they lived in huts "up in the hills of Japan."[4] He had met another Japanese man that day, he wrote, who had lived in Los Angeles for more than thirty years and who "spoke English very good for a Jap."

"This country is very beautiful, where I am," Marty added. "The clouds are below us. You can see them pass way down in the valley."

There was, it seemed, a different sort of battle beginning to wage within Marty, one between that which he had been told—had read and heard and seen all around him both at home and abroad, which had been relentlessly drilled into him, which he had absorbed into his very being as a matter of survival—and what he was experiencing firsthand, on a human level, with women who bowed and men who saluted and those who showed as much curiosity about him as he did about them.

A dirty race, a beautiful country. Which was true, and which false?

In his hut above the clouds, perhaps the skinny kid from Syracuse with a busted eardrum and a stack of stationery had begun to wonder for himself.

Back in the States, Marty was honorably discharged on May 13, 1946, from a hospital in Portsmouth, New Hampshire, after receiving treatment for appendicitis.[5] With the war over and his military service complete, Marty took the money he hadn't either spent or sent home from his monthly salary of sixty-six dollars and traveled to Syracuse by train. He walked along Strathmore Drive toward his house as the clock passed midnight.

Marty's family knew he was coming; his seabag had beaten him here. What they didn't know was exactly when. He hoped to surprise them, but the front door was locked, and so was the side door. Marty rang the bell. After a few moments, a light clicked on inside, and then his brother Joe was at the door. His younger sisters came bounding down the stairs, his parents close behind. Marty couldn't believe how much his youngest sister had grown. It had been nearly three years since he'd seen any of them.

The only one who didn't join the homecoming was Skippy, Marty's dog. The tricolored springer spaniel hung back on the stairs, skeptical eyes framed by long ears sizing up this stranger in uniform. Only when Marty knelt down to coax him did Skippy finally recognize him.

The family walked to the kitchen. Marty's seabag lay on the floor. It was so heavy, they told him, that the deliveryman from the railway company needed help from Marty's father and brother just to lug it into the house.

My souvenirs, Marty thought. He opened the bag, eager to show off his prizes—the disassembled Japanese machine gun, the hand grenades, the two Japanese rifles, and the foreign photos, diary, and pay records.

His parents chuckled and reminded him it was the middle of the night. "Let's look tomorrow morning," they said.

The next morning was Sunday, so Marty and his family went to mass, as they had every week before he left and while he was gone. Instead of reading prayers by moonlight in a foxhole, Marty was in a wooden pew, surrounded by his family, expected to assimilate to civilian life as if he hadn't just experienced the trauma of war overseas before he could even legally order a beer back home.

After church, Marty unpacked his bag. The diary and letters, in their mysterious script, were of no use to him. If someone came to visit, he would show off the papers, grenades, or rifle if they were interested, in a sense proving to himself and his guests that he really had been there. He really had been in the fight.

Marty did try on the white shirt he'd taken from a dead Japanese soldier on the west side of the island. He thought maybe he could wear it. But it didn't fit. It went in a drawer with the rest of the souvenirs.

And Marty went on with his life.

How much Marty and the countless other souvenir takers knew regarding the significance assigned to the objects they coveted is lost to history. Were they aware of the spiritual meaning behind the items, not just in death but in life? Did they understand that senninbari belts were there to protect, the flags to inspire, each offering a piece of home? Did American materialism come first, enhanced by the natural tendency to assign value and traits to inanimate objects—or did they know about the fuller importance, making the perceived value of the object that much greater?

Were they collecting or stealing?

Either way, one significance was replaced by another. The belief in protection, the reminders of home and family and honor, were now pieces in collections, exotic, covet-worthy objects obtained by virtue of the triumph over a hated enemy in a faraway land.

For some, even many, souvenir hunting in the Pacific Theater contained elements of malicious thievery. But to explain the *why*, perhaps there was a more straightforward reason that had less to do with conscious choice and more to do with the natural mechanisms of the human brain.

The compulsion to collect is in our very wiring, an animal-level instinct akin to second nature. It's hard for most people to relate to the idea of killing another human being, especially face to face, and then looting the body of that person. But at some point in our lives, we've all been collectors: of rocks or baseball cards or bits and pieces, of lightning bugs in jars or newspaper clippings or stamps or coins.

Surrounded by death, their fates out of their own hands—and yes, without question, conditioned to view the Japanese enemy as less than and subhuman—these young men likely experienced "neurological forces at play" in their brains that lit up to say *collect*.[6]

The brain, both the most fascinating and least understood human organ, is under constant assault in any battlefield. The cerebral cortex—our gray matter—has four lobes that are responsible for everything from rational thought and decision-making to memory, personality, and emotions.[7] The nucleus accumbens, or pleasure center, and the amygdala, or fear center, work in tandem with other parts of the brain when choices are on the line. Thanks to modern scientific imagery, researchers now understand "that the drive to collect is rooted in our neurobiology."[8]

All of this was heightened to an extreme in the Pacific, where macabre collections of belongings were created under the most intense circumstances.

"Psychologists have studied this, by the way," writes science journalist and author Lulu Miller, "the sweet salve that collecting can offer in times of anguish." In her book, *Why Fish Don't Exist*, she points to Werner Muensterberger, a psychologist who determined "that the habit often kicks into high gear after some sort of 'deprivation or loss or vulnerability,'" and to the research of Francisca López-Torrecillas, at the University of Granada, who "noted a similar phenomenon, that people experiencing stress or anxiety would turn to collecting to soothe their pain."[9]

The "otherness" of the souvenirs would also have ignited the part of the brain associated with novelty. "It responds to the new and is awash with dopaminergic neurons," writes neuroscientist (and avid art collector) Shirley Mueller, "which are part of the reward system and can influence behavior. Stimulation of this center can lead to additional exploration in anticipation of a further reward."[10]

The writer John Hersey, while embedded with the US Marines during a 1942 campaign in the dense jungle of Guadalcanal, came upon a physical object—a discarded head net—that was his first sign of the as-yet-hidden Japanese forces. His brain fired off several messages at once: a realization of the enemy as an actual person, a sense of novelty, and an impulse to keep the item. "This thing in my hand, this symbol of the animal wiles our men find so hard to understand, brought me for the first time face to face with the enemy as an individual, not just as an idea," Hersey wrote in *Into the Valley*.[11] He had "long hated the idea," but he realized that his hatred did not extend to the individual. How could it? That singular person had never wronged him.

Hersey's journalistic mind flashed with questions, though they were less about fact-finding and more about genuine human curiosity. Was the owner of this item from the colder north or the warmer south of Japan? What did the "arrogant characters on the little flag he was to carry to the front" say? How much of his rice rations were cooked or uncooked? Had the "Emperor's praises [rung] in his skull" before he scaled this tree, before he bailed and ran, before he left his head net behind? His curiosity winning out, Hersey picked up the abandoned souvenir and placed it over his own helmet.

As a self-protective measure, the brain also conditions itself into rationalizing an action that the person might not otherwise have taken. A kind of "self-talk" known as cognitive consistency, according to Mueller, can help someone "overlook the negative and emphasize the positive internally to resolve [a] conflict. . . . It is human to use this kind of mental process within ourselves when we allow desire to reign over moral and ethical considerations and attempt to reconcile the conflict."[12]

It was also, on a basic level, a phenomenon called the "herding effect"—mob mentality. To put it simply, everyone was doing it. (In reality, not everyone was doing it, but enough were to make that seem true.) The competitive nature and testosterone levels of young men under intense circumstances likely overrode whatever moral questions they might otherwise have pondered.

When we collect something, the brain's pleasure center is stimulated, proven to light up on functional magnetic resonance imaging. "But interestingly enough," notes Mueller, "the pleasure center doesn't burn as brightly when we get what we want, as when we *imagine* what we'd want."[13] In other words: the brain loves the thrill of the chase.

The instinct for survival must have been triggered. The more souvenirs you collect, the more kills you've made, the longer you're alive. That's one less enemy to fight, meaning the closer the war is to ending and the closer you are to going home. There must also have been an eagerness to show off souvenirs to fellow Marines or sailors or soldiers, and as trophies back in America, boosting your dreams of home and family and comfort, though at times the dream seemed impossible to fathom.

Whatever the motivations, they likely morphed over time. For those who lived to see their futures beyond the battlefield, the original force behind the action of bending down and looting a dead body of personal belongings probably no longer existed as it had back in that moment.

And then what?

Details from the first few days after Marty's return home are lost to all but the walls of the house on Strathmore Drive. Perhaps his parents were concerned about what they saw, despite page after page of V-Mail telling them not to worry. The kid from Syracuse was still skinny, though more grown-up in ways they could not have imagined. Could they see what he'd been through in his eyes, in the way he carried himself, in a jumpiness that hadn't been there before? Perhaps they asked him why he'd brought so many foreign trinkets home, the personal belongings of dead enemies, some with handwriting none of them could understand. Did they even want those cursed things in their house, constant reminders of the war?

Perhaps they asked him how the items had come into his possession. Did he tell the truth in that moment? To the victors went the spoils, and time had not yet settled deeply enough to bring with it doubts, questions, guilt.

The fact is he had the souvenirs. This could not be changed. The killing and collecting were done.

Marty was smarting, though he tried not to show it. He'd had a pretty girlfriend named Mary Lou, and they had seemed very much in love when he'd joined the Marines. Throughout the war, they diligently exchanged correspondence. Marty often asked about her in letters to his parents and brother. He planned to pick up where they'd left off. But upon his return from overseas, Marty received a letter from Mary Lou telling him she'd met someone else.

Marty was a veteran, a local war hero, a survivor of Iwo Jima. A "Dear John" letter was a blow to the ego, sure, but he was young and handsome, and this was not going to ruin his summer. Not when he was back home, at last, and alive. He might not have had marriage on the mind just then, being barely twenty years old, but he knew what he was looking for. He'd find it where he least expected.

Marty went to work at a drugstore called Ostrom's. His uncle, sick with cancer, owned the place, so Marty helped him out as a soda jerk. One day he noticed a group of girls in the store. One of them had caught his eye even before he left for the war, while he was still dating Mary Lou. She was beautiful and polite. *Very wholesome*, he had thought. *I'm going to marry that girl.*

Each time she came into the shop, Marty made sure to wait on her. Her name was Janet Walsh, she was from the south side of town, and she was younger than he, only fifteen or sixteen. He also knew that her father was a very large man.[14] Marty trod carefully but diligently. When he worked up the nerve to call Janet for the first time, he used the excuse to ask the time of her novena at church. "He just wanted me to know what a nice boy he was," she later said with a laugh.

The day she walked into the drugstore with a tennis racquet, Marty knew he had a chance. "Oh, you play tennis?" he asked, despite the obvious answer. He took her to Kirk Park, where their first official date occurred on the clay courts, though neither was all that good at the sport. (The couple later developed a lifelong love of the game, which culminated in their building a tennis court at their home.)

Their courtship was pleasant, and they enjoyed each other's company. They played tennis on the weekends or went camping. Marty loved how positive Janet was, always fun to be around and keeping him on his toes—even after three or four dates, when Marty was still waiting for his first goodnight kiss. Marty told Janet he was going to get a kiss at the end of their date. That night, she shut the screen door in his face.

Marty was in love. After everything he had been through, it was exactly what he needed.

In Janet, Marty had met his match. Behind the easygoing smile he loved so much was a competitive and sharp mind, a sense of humor, and a love of pranks that rivaled his own. But

Marty and Janet
(courtesy Connor family)

the teenage Janet was not immune to what people thought, and the girl who grew up on the other side of town thrilled when Marty arrived in a convertible to pick her up from the pool where she worked as a swim instructor. It made all the other girls jealous—the same girls who used to offer to give her a ride home just to make fun of where she lived and the house she grew up in.

Janet was born on July 19, 1931, to Leo and Mary Rose Walsh.[15] She had three siblings, including a twin brother, James. The kids spent summers on Tupper Lake, in the Adirondacks, with their aunts. Janet thought Marty was awfully cute, and she thought he was younger than he actually was, at least at first, because even after his service in the war, he still looked like a teenager.

By 1950, Marty was a student on the GI Bill, part of the first class at Le Moyne College, a Jesuit university in Syracuse. Janet, after graduating as high school valedictorian, had enrolled in nursing school at St. Joseph's on a scholarship. The New York Yankees had bested the Brooklyn Dodgers in the World Series the previous fall. "Rag Mop" by the Ames Brothers was at the top of the charts, and *All the King's Men* would take Best Picture at the Academy Awards. The brutality of the Pacific seemed like a different lifetime.

Just months before Marty's graduation, the Marines came calling. A different fight was ramping up in the Pacific, and Marty's services were required once more. He was sent back to Parris Island, this time as a drill instructor, training recruits headed to the front lines of the Korean War. Marty relished being back in the Corps. He dreamed of returning to Le Moyne, graduating, and becoming an officer. He wanted to make a career as a Marine.

Perhaps he felt most at home bringing order to experiences that were nearly impossible to process, with like-minded people who could also understand how it had been. Coming home after the war, where did he fit in? How does a young boy, now a man, having gone through the most formative years of his life under unfathomable conditions, reenter civilian life and be expected to pick up where he left off?

Post-traumatic stress disorder (PTSD) only came to be known as such in the 1980s, but that does not mean it didn't exist before then.[16] Instead, it went by other names, such as "shell shock" and "combat exhaustion," terms that largely downplayed a psychiatric trauma response deserving of a proper medical diagnosis. Many veterans of the Second World War chose to deal with their trauma

Marty Connor, 1951 (courtesy Connor family)

by not dealing with it at all, mostly burying their experiences and rarely speaking of them. Over time, Marty would take the opposite approach, though some things he still kept close.

Ultimately, his military dreams were not to be. Six months into Marty's work at Parris Island, his father suddenly died, leaving behind Marty's mom, his siblings, and the family business. In his mid-twenties, Marty returned home to take over the insurance company and take care of his family. Still, his relatively short time in uniform would shape the rest of his life, playing out personally where it could not happen professionally.

On January 30, 1954, Marty Connor and Janet Walsh married in Syracuse. True to form, for their honeymoon Marty took Janet on a tour of Gettysburg. Perhaps the only thing he

Marty and Janet at their wedding (courtesy Connor family)

loved more than the Marines was Janet, and she loved him right back. Why else would a beautiful young woman agree to spend her honeymoon not on a warm beach somewhere far from the snow and freezing wind of Central New York, but bundled up in a camel-hair trench coat exploring old battlefields? Or pick up a hunting rifle and accompany her husband on pheasant- and duck-hunting adventures? Or attend Marine Corps reunions in cities all over the United States, and eventually even overseas?

Her love was strong enough for her to put up with his obsession with the Marines, one born of unfulfilled dreams and diverted by obligation.

Their first house was on Geddes Street, in the Strathmore area of Syracuse near where Marty grew up. It had three bedrooms, lots of light, and a kennel out back for the dogs. The first six children came in two clusters of three (Shane, Mary, and Martin; then Brian, Terrence, and Daniel), turning the Irish American couple into a family of eight. In 1967, Marty bought a plot of land on Onondaga Hill, in the relative middle of nowhere, to construct a larger home. There would be one more child, Colleen, and now they were a family of nine.

All that time, Iwo Jima was never far behind Marty. At some point, sleeping troubles began. He would wake with a start in the middle of the night, heart pounding. Even during the day, in the light, he'd catch his mind returning to that place. He'd have periods of time when he couldn't sleep at all, his mind replaying what he'd seen and heard and done. Though he was a world away from that volcanic rock in the Pacific, it was as if a piece of him remained there. Maybe it always would.

Meanwhile, the physical pieces—the souvenirs—remained in his home, first on Geddes Street and then on Onondaga Hill.

Still, the Connor home was filled with laughter. Marty and Janet shared a love of pranks, the two conspiring and giggling like schoolchildren when pulling one off. Marty had been a prankster for as long as anyone could remember, and not even the Marine Corps could drill it out of him. In a pack of letters he sent home from the Parris Island barracks in November 1943, he asked his mother to deworm his beloved dog, Skippy ("I think the worm pills are in the silver pot on the left hand side of the buffet," he wrote).[17] On another page, addressed to his brother, he provided less helpful instructions:

> Dear Joe,
> I received your letter about fifteen minutes ago and decided to [answer] it right away. So here goes.
> To worm Skippy, you hold his head back and stroke his throat gently and at the same time drop in four nice worms. One for each ten lbs. Repeat this treatment every 48 hours until the dog starts to crawl like a worm.
> Tell mother that you can have my clothes. I won't be using them for quite some time. I was glad to hear that mother hung Skippy's picture up, where did mom get the frame from, she didn't take some other picture out of its frame did she?
> I am the best looking Marine in bottom bunk no. 17. Our barracks is a one story affair. Which is hot as hell in the day time and as cold as the north pole at night.
> Every night, everything wet freezes up, the windows frost up, and all the puddles of water around this wonderful place have ice on them in the morning.
> I haven't written in a couple days, because I had two more shots and they took all my energy away. Right after we got

our shots, they marched us, and before we had marched a half
hour, there were over twenty fellows <u>out cold</u>, they just left them
lying there in the sand. I felt a little dizzy, but I took it.

It has taken a little time, but I have finally got the Marine
Corp running smooth. Well I shall sign off. Write again soon.

Your brother,

Bud

Marty also had a strict side. His son Dan remembered that
Marty ran the house the only way he knew how: "like a Marine
battalion," largely mirroring the type of household Marty himself had grown up in. There were push-up contests and bedside
prayers performed on your knees while being observed by your
parents. You finished your dinner whether you liked it or not, and
if you were one of the five boys, your hair was buzz cut with clip-
pers, courtesy of your father.

Colleen, Marty and Janet's youngest, was scared of her father
for the first sixteen years of her life, give or take a few. He was
a Marine in every sense of the word, hard on her older siblings,
especially her brothers. They engaged in typical teenage shenan-
igans, but Marty the insurance man had little patience for rule
breaking when it came to his kids.

And good luck if you were trying to date one of Marty Connor's daughters. He was "horrible" to Colleen's boyfriends, cleaning his guns and knives on the kitchen table anytime she had a
date. On a Friday night not even remotely close to hunting season, he would place them on the table in full view. If Marty didn't
like the guy, he wouldn't even bother looking him in the eye. But
he always made sure his handshake was the firmest.

The old wooden kitchen table seemed to be the center of family life at the house on the hill. Any gathering of friends or family converged there, including Marty's Marine buddies, who visited a few times a year. Colleen remembered one night when she was in her early twenties. She was living at home while contemplating going to law school. A group of war buddies, including her father's best friend, Donny Moyer, were around the table with strange looks on their faces.

Janet pulled Colleen aside. Colleen's cat, Puffer, had died, her mother told her gently. Colleen had had the cat since age six, but the feline smelled terrible, and Marty, a dog person, never even acknowledged Puffer's existence.

The men in the kitchen stared at Colleen, waiting for her response. Then they told her that they had found Puffer's body and had buried the cat in the woods by a pine tree because they didn't want Colleen to see her like that, or to have to perform the burial herself.

It was one of many ways that Marty, usually so stoic and reserved, demonstrated that underneath the outer shell resided an emotional guy. Most of his friends were the same.

As years went by, Colleen and her brother Dan, the second youngest, began to see a different side of their father, one that was less like a drill instructor. Colleen recalled a particular turning point for Marty—a mellowing out, an apparent sense of peace—after an event that began with a phone call.

The call was an invitation to return to Iwo Jima.

CHAPTER 6

He knew every crest, every divot, every hole. Thirty-six traumatic days on Iwo Jima had etched them in his mind forever. But this was new. Marty had never seen Iwo from here, from the sky.

The plane swooped around Mount Suribachi, its silver wings tipping as if in salute.[1] Marty pressed his camcorder to the window, the images imprinting on film just as they had on his brain two and a half decades ago.

It was the twenty-fifth anniversary of the battle. This time, Janet was with him. He ran through a mental checklist of all the prominent spots he wanted to show her: the foxholes where he'd dug in for the night, the places where he'd dodged mortar fire, the exact location where he'd first stepped on the beach.

It was February 19, 1970. Not long before, the phone had rung at Marty's house in Syracuse. It was Charles Early, a fellow

Fifth Marine Division veteran. There's a reunion happening on Iwo, he told Marty. Was he ready to return?

Twenty-five years earlier, Charles E. Early had been an eighteen-year-old private in the 31st Replacement Battalion. On Iwo Jima, he was assigned to a rifle company, which landed on D-Day plus one, February 20, 1945. Just shy of three weeks later, while engaged in a heavy firefight against the Japanese, Charles was darting across an open area to get more stretchers for the wounded. A bullet from a Japanese sniper hit him in his right side, piercing his hip and abdomen. William Shadley, another brave Marine, ran into the open area and pulled Charles to safety.

Charles would spend the next sixteen months in several naval hospitals, from Guam to Bethesda. For ten months, he lay in a body cast to relocate his hip. The injury would leave him with a permanent limp and ruin his dreams of a career in the Marines. But as with Marty, Iwo was a constant presence in his life and the lives of his family. Charles met his wife, Bonnie, while in recovery at Bethesda Naval Hospital. They had two children, Chuck and Mary, who were never allowed to use derogatory terms like "Jap." Though their father had been badly wounded by the Japanese, to the point of being unable to tie his shoe or put a sock on his right foot, Charles did not blame them. "They were doing their job, and I was doing mine," he would tell his children.

Charles credited his somewhat unusual empathy toward the Japanese to his acting commander, Lieutenant Karl Tanner, who ordered his Marines not to mistreat any of the Japanese prisoners they might take during the battle.[2] "The war was over for these men, and they should be treated like human beings," Charles remembered Tanner saying. "They had been our allies before the war and could be our friends again someday." Those words stuck with young Charles, and more than twenty years later, when the opportunity for a reunion with Japanese Iwo survivors presented itself, Charles latched on.

For three years, turning the opportunity into reality would become his greatest obsession.[3]

It was not easy.

Charles traveled to Japan in 1967, three years before the anniversary, in an attempt to contact Japanese veterans of the battle. There were so few of them, and some of those who remained lived in hiding, unable to face the shame of having surrendered or been defeated, preferring that their families believe them to be dead.

Because of that disgrace, many of the widows of Japanese soldiers killed on the island refused to meet the survivors, even all those years later. Charles sidestepped these politics by coming to an agreement with both parties: the Japanese veterans would be on the island on February 19, and the widows could meet the American veterans the next day at a separate event.

The logistics were another problem. Ironically, considering that the battle was fought primarily over Iwo's airstrips, the Japanese said that no plane was available to get the veterans from Tokyo to Iwo Jima.

"It seems like Iwo Jima is the most difficult place to go to in the world," Charles wrote in a letter sent to members of the Fifth Marines on July 29, 1969.[4] "We expected our first trip there to be difficult, but we certainly never expected the second one to be so much trouble."

Charles negotiated once more, this time with the help of President Richard Nixon's White House. A US Air Force plane would transport the American group from mainland Japan to the black sand beaches of Iwo.

The reunion was on.

At five in the morning on February 19, 1970, the Marines and their families gathered at Tachikawa Airfield for the flight to Iwo Jima. Food packets were provided for the journey.[5] The borrowed plane circled the island before its descent, affording passengers a glimpse at both how much and how little had changed. It landed on one of the precious airstrips that had first drawn interest from the Allied forces command—and thus had drawn the Marines to the island in 1945. A delegation of Japanese veterans arrived in a silver military aircraft of their own, emblazoned on the side with a vibrant red circle.

Janet held the video camera as Marty stepped onto the black beach, which was surrounded by brilliant blue waves that were swallowed by the sand at water's edge. Marty looked like a Kennedy in his dark suit, crisp white shirt, and thin black tie, his caramel hair tousled by the wind.

He knelt and clutched a fistful of sand. The dark granules filtered through his fingers and dispersed in the breeze. When Marty had first been here, when he first saw this beach, it was littered with bodies dead and dying, with blood and bullets, with chaos. Only a teenager, he couldn't picture himself walking off the island alive. Now he had returned as a man, as a husband, as a father.

Janet watched him through the viewfinder of the video camera. In a chic black dress and white head scarf, she was doing her best Jackie O. She now stood on the same beach Marty had landed on all those years ago, in the place that had played such a pivotal role in shaping the man she loved. It was here that Marty, only eighteen years old, had seen his first dead bodies, two American Marines slumped in a crater in the sand that had been formed by a shell explosion. Both had bled out, their bodies the ashen gray of death. It was where he first thought to himself, *Connor, what the hell are you doing here?*

A smattering of American and Japanese media were present to cover the event, including NBC News international correspondent John Rich. Rich himself had fought at Iwo Jima as a member of the 4th Marine Division. He'd learned to speak Japanese at the Navy Language School and perfected it with a posting in Tokyo after the war as a correspondent for the International News Service.[6] On this day, he helped serve as translator between the American and Japanese veterans.

Rich listened as a Japanese survivor of Iwo, who had emerged during the battle from the vast networks of fortified caves to surrender to US forces, spoke to an American vet. "He says, he thanks the Americans very much for taking care of him when he came out," Rich translated.

The American man nodded. "After animosity against the Japanese," he replied, "I have nothing but admiration for your people and especially the defenders of Iwo Jima."

It didn't take long before the former enemies began reliving the battle using maps. Charles Early had his family with him, including his son, Chuck, and daughter, Mary. They posed for photographs, including one taken in front of the base operations building, where a white sign read in bold black letters, "Iwo Jima Airbase, Field Elevation 353 ft." in both English and Japanese.

Some of the Americans and their families wandered the island, picking up shrapnel fragments as souvenirs or bottling up bits of black sand. Others, like Marty, revisited prominent locations from the battle. John Rich observed, "The long, black landing beach looked as treacherous as ever. Its shifting volcanic sands long ago swallowed up the debris of battle. Atop Mount Suribachi, there's an American memorial where the famous flag-raising took place. Other than these unmistakable landmarks, however, the island itself seems strangely changed."[7]

The Americans had returned Iwo Jima to Japan two years earlier. And where it had been barren and windy during the battle itself, vegetation now covered much of the island. Yet many of the unmistakable elements of Iwo remained beneath the fresh ground cover. Suribachi still loomed like a giant, casting its shadow over the island's pork-chop shape.

This was not just a reunion for the Marines. The delegation of thirty-seven American veterans and some of their wives and children were here to meet Japanese veterans—some of the few who survived the invasion—and their families. It was a profound step not just politically, for two countries only twenty-five years removed from a hateful, bitter conflict, but personally, for those who fought and for their relatives who grieved, then and now. Standing face to face, shoulder to shoulder, were people who all loved and worried about and provided for their families. The meeting was as important in many ways for the family members, who harbored their own views of the war and the enemy, as it was for the veterans themselves.

It was important to Marty that Janet experience this with him. She was, in all ways, his partner. And it was here that the most formative experience of his life had taken place. Now she could see it too—could hear the waves and smell the sulfur emitted by the volcanic island and touch the black sand. This time, he would not have to bear the emotional burden alone. He could step forward with her by his side, and possibly even begin to heal.

The meeting would take place on the summit of Suribachi itself, the 554-foot extinct volcano at the southwest end of the island. It was the spot where Joe Rosenthal snapped his famous flag-raising photograph for the Associated Press that would become a seminal image of the war and later be memorialized

Marty and Janet on Iwo Jima, February 1970
(courtesy Connor family)

in bronze as the Marine Corps War Memorial in Arlington, Virginia.

As the visiting party made its way up the mountain, Janet looked back toward the water. She could not imagine how Marty had made it through alive.[8] From her vantage point, the Japanese guns were pointed directly down on that beach. Aimed exactly at Marty.

On top of Mount Suribachi, a line of Japanese veterans stood waiting. Marty and his fellow Marines, the victors of this tiny island, walked down the line, shaking hands one by one with the very men they once fought against. With each greeting, Marty and the others bowed their heads in respect. The American veterans were taller than their Japanese counterparts. They struck imposing figures, but Marty never felt any animosity that day. It was a time for reflection and appreciation. *They suffered and we suffered*, Marty thought. *We aren't that different in the end.*

Janet captured it all on film. Her video camera caught Marty taking photos of the beaches. A little Japanese boy in a red jumper stood behind him, curious about this American stranger. Janet smiled at the young Japanese women who were toting babies; she could relate.

Like Marty, she thought the similarities were striking: *We aren't that different in the end.*

Later, once back in Tokyo, she would be seated next to a Japanese woman whose husband had died on Iwo Jima. The woman, just like Janet, was a nurse. Across from her sat a young boy whose father had died on Iwo Jima.

"If I had been on the other side of that table," Janet reflected years later, "I know how I would have felt."

That evening, back home in the United States, *NBC Nightly News* ran a special report filed by John Rich. Anchor David Brinkley, wearing a light gray suit, returned from a commercial break and told his viewers, "World War II was twenty five years ago. But this week, at opposite ends of the earth, some of its memories were revived. Yesterday, in Munich, Germany, a funeral for seven elderly Jews killed in a fire in their community center. On Iwo Jima in the Pacific, the Japanese and the Americans got together and decided they were no longer enemies."[9]

The report included video from the top of Mount Suribachi, where men in pressed white uniforms had hoisted two flags up poles that stood side by side. The red, white, and blue stars and stripes snapped in the breeze next to the red circle on white fabric, the wind blowing the two in the same direction, together.

Of everyone Marty and Janet saw that day, a man in black had caught their eye. A Buddhist monk, he stood out from the crowd, tall and thin and bald, his robes trailing behind him in the wind. In front of him, like a shield, he carried a large brown hat that came to a point. His name was Tsunezo Wachi.

Following an organized lunch held in Tokyo after the ceremony, Marty spoke to the monk. In perfect English, Wachi told Marty that he had been returning personal items recovered from the battlefield to families of dead Japanese soldiers. One of the Marines at the reunion had brought some souvenirs with him that he'd taken during the war. The monk had been able to identify the original owner and had tracked down the surviving Japanese family, who traveled a full day by train to make it to Tokyo before the American delegation left Japan.

At the airport, Marty watched as the dead soldier's tearful parents met the Marine and accepted their son's personal belongings. They appeared so grateful. It had all been facilitated by Wachi. Something in Marty clicked into place.

Immediately, he thought of his own souvenirs, the diary and pay records, the photographs and letters, collecting dust in his drawer at home. Twenty-five years before, he had taken them from the bodies of Japanese soldiers, as so many Marines, soldiers, and sailors had, often only moments after death. They were tokens, prizes, evidence that Marty had been to this place, fought this battle, survived.

Now he saw them in a different light. He witnessed, there in front of him, the impact the seemingly trivial artifacts could have. It was spiritual, Wachi explained. Most of the Japanese families had no bodies to bury. Many of them never even knew when and where their loved ones had died, crucial pieces of information when it came to funeral rites in Japanese Buddhism.[10] For the deceased, an article representing them in life was crucial for their afterlife.[11] These recovered belongings could be offered to the family altar, and at long last the departed souls would be at peace.

Buddhism arrived in Japan with Korean immigrants in the sixth century. Like so much coming from outside the island nation's borders, it was at first received with much skepticism. It would take some two hundred years before Buddhism was adopted as the state religion under Emperor Shōmu, who ruled from 724 to 749, during the Nara period.[12] Influences from China bolstered the faith, especially after Japan's imperial capital city was moved in 794 from Nara to Heian-kyō—the city known today as Kyoto.

Though its role as the seat of government and the emperor's residence would end with the beginning of the Meiji Restoration in 1868, ancient Kyoto was, as it remains today, Japan's cultural and religious heart.[13] An estimated two thousand temples currently stand in the city, the spires of their pagoda rooftops piercing the skyline. The majority are Buddhist temples of many different sects, followed in number by shrines dedicated to Shintō, the religion native to Japan. With its blended focus on culture and religion, the city fostered a level of unrivaled craftsmanship to support the growing religious institutions and their respective places of worship.

In Kyoto's Shichijo neighborhood, as early as the eleventh century, the fabrication of Buddhist altar fittings—such as statues, incense holders, and other items—took on a life of its own.[14] The craftsmen did not create the whole, but rather specialized in the individual, each of their steps building on the last to construct elaborate temples adorned with gold.

As time went on, and lives got busier, and populations grew and became less centralized, families began to erect butsudan: miniatures of temples, designed and personalized for the home. Butsudan became more popular in the seventeenth century, first in Kyoto and then fanning out to the rest of the country.[15] The temple craftsmen scaled down their works of art, applying the same meticulous commitment to each element of the butsudan.

The kijishi (wood joiner), perched on a thin cushion and hunched over a low table, coaxes each individual piece of wood into the base of the altar without using a single nail. The

A butsudan (photo:
Patrick Bresnahan)

horishi (wood-carver), surrounded by delicate shavings, works
to depict scenes on the flat surfaces of doors or on an ornately
carved header for the top of the altar. The nushi (lacquerer)
applies urushi lacquer, most typically in black, though sometimes in a shade of red or brown, providing a vibrant base for
the ever-important next step. The hakuoshishi (gold-leaf dec-
orator), using hundreds of sheets of impossibly thin gold leaf,
so delicate it can melt into the hand with barely any pressure
or flutter away at the slightest breath, applies gilt to the walls,
pillars, and interior sanctum of the butsudan. The busshi (Buddhist sculptor), responsible for "bringing the wood to life," prac-
tices the sacred art of carving the Buddha. The roiroshi (wax
polisher) makes the deep black of the urushi lacquer shine like a

mirror, applying a combination of charcoal pieces and white powdered deer antler with his palm. The saishikishi (color painter) renders vibrant scenes on the wood base or gold leaf. The makieshi (lacquer artist), after ensuring that the urushi lacquer has cured at just the right humidity and temperature, uses gold powder to craft intricate designs. The kirikaneshi (gold thread artist) cuts sheer strips of gold foil using a deerskin stand and bamboo knife. The kazarikanagushi (decorative metal fitter) adds gold fixtures. The chokinshi (gold engraver), with his tagane (chisel), taps out a rhythm "as if playing a melody."[16] In fact, a full orchestra is involved, making an individual yet cohesive effort to create the most personal place of worship for each family.

As time went by, the purpose of the butsudan expanded. It became not just a temple at home and a place to worship the Buddha and the divinities that were part of a family's sect, but a place to remember and honor one's ancestors, a place to enshrine their souls, to give thanks to them and provide rest for them.[17] Often set in a room of great importance, situated so family members could kneel before it on tatami mats and offer prayer and reflection, the traditional butsudan might be as large as a wardrobe, with drawers to hold offerings to those who had passed and surfaces to light incense. It was with personal offerings on behalf of the deceased relatives that the monk Tsunezo Wachi was trying to help. When stolen belongings were returned to the family of a loved one who had died, the empty place on the altar could be filled. A soul could rest at last.

Much like the butsudan itself, Wachi's mission would require both an individual and a collective effort, one that was meticulous and delicate and beautiful. Bearing responsibility for eternal souls required a sacrifice of Wachi's own emotional peace, a debt he felt he needed to repay time and time again, though he surely did not share this sentiment upon first meeting Marty at the reunion. Yet Marty would later learn that Iwo Jima meant something more to Tsunezo Wachi, and the monk would always be haunted by it. This was the price of his own soul, never at rest.

CHAPTER 7

It is very significant to hold such a ceremony together with the Americans and Japanese in such a way on a famous spot. It will contribute to the peace of the Pacific, I firmly believe.

—Tsunezo Wachi

NORTHERN JAPAN / 1945

Chikako Ogawa, fourteen years old, huddled with her classmates around the crackling radio in her school in rural northern Japan. It was noon on August 15, 1945. A high-pitched voice she had never heard spoke words she could not believe.[1] The emperor, leader of Japan's holy war against the United States, used a sophisticated version of the Japanese language.

But there was no vocabulary that could disguise Emperor Hirohito's ultimate message: Japan had lost.

The war was over, the future uncertain.

For Chikako and her family, it meant they could finally return home to Tokyo, from which they had fled during the constant threat of American air raids. A hatred for the enemy burned as hot as the flames from indiscriminate firebombing. Only people with "evil minds" could have done what they did, Chikako reasoned, fearful of what it would mean if the Americans stepped foot in mainland Japan.[2]

It also meant something else: soon, though the family did not know when, her father might return home. Only if, of course, he was still alive, which they did not know for sure.

In preparation, uncertain whether the patriarch would return or what an American-led occupation would entail, Chikako's mother unearthed her textbooks from when she had studied English literature as a college student in Nagasaki.[3] Banned during the war, the books could now become a valuable tool. The future English teacher began with her own children.

They would be ready for the future in whatever form it took.

Chikako's father, Captain Tsunezo Wachi, was indeed alive and ready to see his wife and children again. But there was something he needed to do first. In November 1945, on the train ride home from his posting in Kagoshima, Wachi disembarked early—not in Tokyo, where his family was waiting for him, but in Kyoto. He had escaped death three times during the war. Why had he been spared when so many others were not? The guilt coursed through him, weighed on him, none heavier than the knowledge that he should have been on Iwo Jima with his men the previous February and March, fighting alongside them, likely dying alongside them.

But he had not been there. And the tiny island would loom like a giant for the rest of Wachi's life.

Born in Yamaguchi prefecture on July 24, 1900, Tsunezo Wachi came from a proud Japanese family.[4] Nineteen years later, he enrolled at the Imperial Japanese Naval Academy in Etajima, Hiroshima. The ethos of the time was instilled in him: duty, honor, emperor. A knack for communication skills sent him to the Naval War College in April 1926, to specialize in learning Spanish. Three months later, he was married.

A young Tsunezo Wachi
(courtesy Rosa
Chikako Ogawa)

His career and family blossomed. He spent several years in China as a communications officer, coding and decoding messages, before receiving a special assignment. In November 1940, he traveled to Mexico City to become the new assistant naval attaché, putting his Spanish and English language skills to good use. His "confidential real mission," he would later write, "was to set up an intelligence communication station." They called it the "L system"—one letter ahead of *M* for Mexico—and set about spying on the US fleet in the Atlantic.

It was there, just over a year later, that he would intercept a message sent from the American forces in Hawaii. The two short lines, he'd write almost four decades later, were words he'd never forget: "Air raid on Pearl. This is not a drill."

Wachi read that message with dread. Having spent time observing the United States and gathering intelligence, he was fully aware of its military capabilities and resources. Privately—for one could never speak out of turn against the empire—Wachi feared a drawn-out conflict that would mean endless suffering and inevitable defeat.

Still, Japan was not without its own firepower. During the Meiji Restoration, which began in 1868, the country took inspiration from the West to modernize and transform itself on both the industrial and military fronts.[5] Japan flexed its military might throughout Asia, steamrolling and colonizing its Pacific neighbors from Korea to parts of China to the Philippines. By the 1930s, Japan's aggression into Manchuria and later mainland China would send relations with the United States into a downward spiral that culminated in a 1941 American embargo on oil shipments to Japan—a source of the precious resource that, by then, had made up 80 percent of the country's oil imports.[6] The breakdown between Japan and other countries spread to Great Britain and the Netherlands.[7]

A hypermilitarized, nationalist, imperial Japan decided on its sole course of action: all-out war. This led to the attack on Pearl Harbor, a public declaration of war against the United States and its allies. The Pacific soon became engulfed in conflict, which left a trail of collateral damage in its wake.

As 1943 drew to a close, and with Japan "on the verge of her catastrophe," Wachi wrote, "I didn't feel like sitting at a desk performing communication duties anymore. I wanted to prove myself a military man."

He requested a transfer, and his wish was granted in early 1944. "We are going to set up a new Garrison squad on Iwo Jima," a member of the naval personnel department told him over the phone. The navy would oversee the defense of the island, with army troops as reinforcements. "We made an agreement with them that you are to be the Garrison Commander General."

At age forty-three, Wachi was an experienced and well-traveled naval officer, but he lacked combat expertise. Doubt crept in as he flew from Kisarazu Air Base in Chiba prefecture, east of Tokyo, to the inhospitable hunk of volcanic rock that was Iwo Jima.

Waiting to assist him were a lieutenant and a "handful of men," Wachi remembered. "I was much obliged because this assistant of mine was efficient enough to help his inexperienced commander." The team got to work, beginning the construction of the island's defensive strongholds in March 1944. Wachi later wrote:

Every ship that arrived was loaded with not only soldiers and sailors but also 25mm anti-aircraft machine guns and shallow-water mines. As far as my previous experience went, they were all totally new to me. Fixing those arms on the island and building up a strong point was just like the work of public engineering.

Most of all those new men were sent by the nation-wide mobilization. So they had never been drafted. They had had no experience in military training. They were just civilians. I discussed the matter with the adjutant and decided that one day a week we would stop the construction work and [teach] them military discipline with the aim that we hold a military parade on April 29, [the] Emperor's birthday to encourage their morale.

By the time the parade was held, the second runway had been completed. On [the] Emperor's birthday about 5,000 army and navy men stood at attention while I inspected and saluted them on horseback. All cheered "Banzai" three times and wished for the recovery from the discouraging situation of the war.

The daily report, however, became more unfavorable for us every day. We were very much afraid that the island would be involved in the bloodshed battle any moment.

Those fears were warranted. Allied forces island-hopped, at considerable cost to both sides, throughout the Pacific, inching ever closer to mainland Japan. By July 1944, Saipan had fallen; in October, Leyte.[8] Iwo's precious runways, Wachi knew, needed to be defended "by all means."

"It was no more a situation for navy alone to take the responsibility of the island defending under only a Garrison commander," Wachi wrote. "The Military Headquarters were to take the command directly as for the defense of the island. General [Tadamichi] Kuribayashi was assigned as commander general and came to the island from Bonin Islands [on June 8, 1944].[9] His new strategy was to 'Destroy them after they are lured to get ashore,' which contradicted the one we had been following. Therefore, there occurred a great dispute between army and navy."

It was the two schools of thought that would come to define strategies in Japan's island defenses, a divide that only worsened an already-festering rivalry between the army and the navy.[10] The first was the forward beachhead concept, which the navy had been following and which had been employed in Guadalcanal in 1942 and Tarawa in 1943: attack at the vulnerable point of entry on the beach before allowing the enemy to advance.

But after the fall of Saipan in July 1944, the military began to question its entire strategy, favoring instead what it called in-depth defense: hunker down in protected and concealed locations, and wait for the enemy to come to you.[11]

The dispute between the two military branches would eventually spell the end of Wachi's leadership—and his time—on Iwo Jima, but not before he would experience daily air raids on the island over the course of summer and into fall, the bombers out of range of the garrison's antiaircraft missiles. "Our headquarters got bombed in the vicinity three times and was partially damaged. On the second time it was bombed I was blown away by the blast and lay unconscious for a while. Fortunately, however, I came to myself. Every night we had to make sure of our survival." Several of Wachi's men in the antiaircraft units were less fortunate, exposed in the bombing runs as they manned guns that could not reach their targets—another point of contention in strategy, this time between Wachi and a naval pilot named Captain Samaji Inoue, who had arrived on the island that summer. The two constantly butted heads over who, exactly, was second in command over Iwo's naval forces.[12]

Then, on October 15, 1944, after eight months on Iwo Jima, what had felt inevitable amid the strategic disputes about the island's defense finally took place. Wachi was transferred back to Yokosuka Naval Station, south of Tokyo. He received a promotion to the rank of captain, but it rang hollow.

Because of the transport schedule, he had to leave the day after receiving the transfer orders. "I didn't even have a split second to

Tsunezo Wachi, garrison commander at Iwo Jima, March 1944 (courtesy Rosa Chikako Ogawa)

bid goodbye to men with whom I had shared my life under severe firing," Wachi later wrote with remorse. "That was the most unwilling transfer I had ever undergone in my navy career."

The fate that awaited his men four months later would make his remorse even harder to bear.

Chikako was running an errand for her mother as afternoon darkened into evening one day in the fall of 1944.[13] In the fading light, a man approached her along the familiar road. He was tall and thin, his uniform worn, his face visibly tanned even in the dark. Only his eyes were "glittering."

Chikako thought she was imagining it. "Dad! Is it you?"

She gawked at him, unable to speak any more words, though there was so much she wanted to say, questions she yearned to ask, concerned over how thin he was.

Wachi looked at his daughter and simply said, "I'm home."

After his unexpected homecoming, Wachi reported to the Imperial Naval headquarters, where he was instructed to take some time to rest and recover. Wachi obeyed but soon became restless. Desperate to serve, he lobbied for a new assignment and was granted another attaché posting, this time in Manila. But the day never came; instead, a new order surfaced.

Wachi was assigned to Kagoshima, near the southern tip of the country, to train kaiten, underwater torpedo pilots similar to kamikaze.[14] His main duty was to convince other young men that theirs was to willingly die for their country, no questions asked.

There, from afar, Wachi learned of the battle at Iwo Jima, the brutality, the loss. His heart broke.[15] A part of him cracked open at the news, at the realization he'd been spared while the men he'd led, leaned on, grown to respect and care for, had almost all been killed.

He had no choice but to keep going, though his assignment training young men to prepare themselves to die weighed on him in the wake of Iwo Jima. The months of spring and early summer 1945 bled into each other until the unthinkable happened: Emperor Hirohito announced the end of the war. Japan had lost; it was done.

Near the end of August, a US Marine battalion led by a Lieutenant Colonel Hayward arrived at Wachi's base in Kagoshima to oversee the takeover and learn everything they could about Japan's plans to defend the mainland against an American invasion. During procedural discussions, Wachi couldn't help himself; his emotions over what he had left behind at Iwo Jima bubbled over. He told Hayward "how sincerely I wished to go back to the island to pray and mourn for the departed souls of all the colleagues, officers and men who had bereaved me."

Hayward, from the position of victor and conquered, regarded the man before him and made an offer: write an appeal to the General Headquarters (GHQ) of the Allied occupation forces for approval to visit the conquered island, and Hayward himself would forward it. It was a gesture that would have been unthinkable only weeks before.

Not long after, it would happen again, when a British liaison officer at GHQ, Colonel Thomas, also visited Kagoshima searching for details about Japan's preparations. Over a meal of curry and rice, Thomas spied Wachi's draft, written in English, requesting his visit to American-held Iwo Jima. "I can make out what you mean," Thomas told Wachi, "but there is room for improvement in English. I'll do it for you if you so wish." On the spot, Wachi remembered, the officer turned his draft into a "beautiful formal application."

Wachi made thirty copies and handed one to Hayward, "who read it thru [*sic*] and stared at me in surprise." Wachi told Hayward about his British assist ("It must have been so," Hayward told him in response. "This is such fine English that I can't even write [it] myself"), feeling confident it would bring his greatest wish to fruition.

Yet perhaps even more poignant, the kindness shown by both men left a lasting impression on Wachi. "Two officers of enemy forces until a few months ago generously offered me their helping hand to make my appeal come to light. I was deeply impressed," Wachi wrote more than forty years later. "It actually marked the very first step of my devotion to the problems of Iwo Jima, and to this day I appreciate the thoughtfulness and friendship rendered me by them right after the dreadful war."

By November 1945, Wachi's official duties were complete. Instead of feeling relieved that he'd survived—and feeling ready to see his family, ready to move on—his mind was stuck on Iwo, where the bodies of more than twenty thousand men remained. Wachi picked up another sheet of paper to draft a plea of a different sort. He wrote a letter to former Japanese reserve officer Lieutenant Kuzuhara, a graduate of Ryukoku Buddhist College, the son of a Buddhist priest, and the heir to his father's temple in Kyoto. Wachi made a request: Could Kuzuhara's father please ordain him?

Kuzuhara met Wachi as he got off the train—not in Tokyo, where his daughter, Chikako, and the rest of his family had returned home to wait for him, but in Kyoto. At the small temple, with its two heavy wooden doors hiding the peaceful green garden inside, the tall Imperial Naval captain with narrow features and a dark mustache told Reverend Kuzuhara of his experiences and declared his intentions, his "responsibility and wish," for Iwo Jima. His goal, Wachi said, was to "perform religious services for the departed souls," though he acknowledged he was "totally ignorant in Buddhism." But he felt compelled to make it happen in the shortest time possible.

"He listened to me with all his heart and said most serenely, 'Your ignorance in the line does not in the least disqualify you from becoming a Buddhist priest. If you have any particular sect of your choice, it may be difficult, but if you prefer our sect, you stay with us about a week making religious practice every day.'" For Wachi, it was no question. He stayed for the week at the Shiunzan Gokurakuin Koshoji Kuyado temple and was ordained a Kuya sect Buddhist priest with the name Jushoan Koami.

"I can't help wondering about the way I was always given a chance of narrow escape from death," he would later write. "All of those [incidents] could have been accidental, but I felt [a] strong power of supernatural providence. It was quite natural for me to retreat from the world to be a Buddhist priest."

The hand of war was only just beginning to cast its long shadow on Japan, its fingers touching all aspects of life: social, economic, political, personal. Wachi and his family would feel all of them in time; no one would be spared. But what Wachi felt most fervently in that moment was the haunting of an "absent presence, by the alternate / universe where they did not make it out," as author Viet Thanh Nguyen has written of survivor's guilt. "What if you were the negative space in / someone else's life and memory?"[16]

It was a question Wachi would wrestle with for the rest of his life, and it possessed him to stop in Kyoto, to change the course of his own future in homage to the past.

He had exchanged his naval uniform for priest's robes, combat boots for plain slippers. Where he once wore captain bars and medals on his chest, he now bore no sign of his military past. It would be another shocking development for his family, who had anxiously awaited the homecoming of Captain Tsunezo Wachi.

Instead, they found a reverend.

Wachi was, to be blunt, a man obsessed. But his desperation to return to Iwo Jima would have to wait. Just six months after his stop in Kyoto to become a man of faith, Wachi landed behind bars in Tokyo's Sugamo Prison. His early war days had come back to haunt him, and he was now being held for questioning—not for what he'd done, but for what he knew. For a month, in a private cell on the first floor of Building Five, he waited.

They gave it a name: the International Military Tribunal for the Far East, though today it is often referred to as the Tokyo War Crimes Trial. It was Japan's version of Nuremberg, the International Military Tribunal in Germany designed to prosecute "the major war criminals of the European Axis."[17] The better-known Nuremberg trials lasted just under a year, from November 20, 1945, to October 1, 1946, during which period twenty-four defendants were tried for crimes against peace, war crimes, and crimes against humanity. Twenty-two would make it to the verdict, which resulted in three acquittals, four prison terms of ten to twenty years each, three life imprisonments, and twelve death sentences, of which ten were carried out on October 16, 1946.[18]

Tokyo's trials would be wider-ranging and last more than two years, involving over eleven hundred witnesses and a court transcript that encompassed almost fifty thousand pages.[19] On January 19, 1946, General Douglas MacArthur, as Supreme Commander for the Allied Powers, issued a special proclamation to establish the tribunal and try those accused of the same three charges as the ones brought at Nuremberg. The charges covered acts stretching from Japan's invasion of Manchuria in 1931 through its surrender in August 1945.[20] Class A charges were crimes against peace, brought against those at the top who had planned and executed the war; class B and C charges comprised war crimes and crimes against humanity.[21]

From May 3, 1946, to November 12, 1948, in a "vast, echoing courtroom" before judges in traditional black robes from countries including the United States, France, Canada, the Soviet Union, China, and the Philippines, nearly thirty Japanese senior political and military leaders would stand trial in Tokyo.[22] The list included wartime general and prime minister Hideki Tojo but, critically, did not include Emperor Hirohito or other members of the imperial family. That was by design, a decision that in many ways continues to impact Japan's postwar reckoning, even today. Not only was the emperor protected from prosecution; he couldn't even be called as a witness during the proceedings, and he was permitted to remain on the throne, by MacArthur himself.

In a telegram to Army Chief of Staff Dwight D. Eisenhower on January 25, 1946, MacArthur made his case.[23] "No specific and tangible evidence has been uncovered with regard to [the

Emperor's] exact activities which might connect him in varying degree with the political decisions of the Japanese Empire during the last decade," MacArthur wrote, a position that has since been widely disputed by historians.[24] MacArthur doubled down, depicting the emperor as a figure who had been unable to "thwart" the militarists who in reality called the shots; if he'd done so, the general continued, Hirohito would have been "in actual jeopardy."

Perhaps most telling, MacArthur stated what it would mean for his own occupational plans if the Allies put someone hailed as divine on trial: "His indictment will unquestionably cause a tremendous convulsion among the Japanese people, the repercussions of which cannot be overestimated. He is a symbol which unites all Japanese. Destroy him and the nation will disintegrate."

Ultimately, Harry Truman, by then the US president, agreed.

On New Year's Day, 1946, Emperor Hirohito made a second historic address. Again, he spoke words the public could not believe. He renounced the "mere legends and myths" that had created "the false conception that the Emperor is divine."[25] In fact, he was just a regular man, no different than his subjects.

All of this made for a confusing message to a population that was reeling from having lost a war and had imbibed nearly a century of propaganda that extolled fighting and dying in the name of the emperor, a divine figure. Unlike Germany, which underwent what journalist Ian Buruma called "a complete break" with the defined entities of the Third Reich and the Nazis following the death of Adolf Hitler—even before Nuremberg—Japan experienced no such disruption with its former identity.[26] And now Emperor Hirohito was absolved.

In May 1946, Wachi was one of 694 people held at Sugamo Prison, a "grim network of squat, ugly, modern buildings of tan concrete, set behind forbidding twenty-foot walls and watchtowers in a quiet residential neighborhood."[27] Its original purpose had been imprisoning political prisoners, which eventually included alleged Allied spies and POWs.

Wachi was grouped under class C—yet he was not there as a war suspect, but rather to testify about what he knew regarding the outbreak of the Pacific War. He was aware of none of this as he sat for weeks in his cell. With the discipline instilled in him from a young age beginning at the Imperial Japanese Naval Academy, Wachi organized his days according to a strict schedule broken into fifteen-minute increments:[28]

0600: Get up
0600–0630: Cleaning room
0630–0700: Reciting the sutras
0700–0715: Breakfast
0715–0730: Sitting quietly
0730–0800: Reciting the sutras
0800–0830: Writing to home
0830–1000: Studying English
1000–1015: Reciting the sutras
1015–1130: Poem-writing
1130–1200: Reciting the sutras
1200–1215: Lunch
1215–1230: Sitting quietly
1230–1300: Reciting the sutras
1300–1400: Reading book
1400–1415: Reciting the sutras
1415–1530: Poem-writing
1530–1545: Reciting the sutras

1545–1645: Reading book
1645–1700: Reciting the sutras
1700–1715: Supper
1715–1730: Sitting quietly
1730–1800: Reciting the sutras
1800–1930: Reading book
1930–2000: Reciting the sutras
2000: Go to bed
> *Change the routine above mentioned for the exercise, bathing and cropping [?], etc, by the suggestion of the American Authority.

Diligently, Wachi composed his poems by agonizing over each individual character until he had the perfect combination, an activity that helped clear his mind. Later he would recall that it enabled him "to overcome all sorts of human desires and shortcomings." The survivor's guilt that had driven him to the steps of the Buddhist temple the year before hovered like a stagnant storm.

Though the arrest warrant that landed him in prison specifically said he was not a suspect of war crimes, the American occupation forces still had questions. Wachi's first hearing took place in June 1946. In the room was "an American gentleman waiting for me with a smile." Having received no information about his arrest, Wachi wasn't in the mood to return any warmth and instead peppered the man with sarcastic questions: "Are you a prosecutor of the Court Martial? What are you going to inquire into just leaving me in the cell for over a month?"

The man, perhaps accustomed to this type of reception by the prisoners, was unfazed. He was not a prosecutor, he told Wachi, but in fact an agent from the US Federal Bureau of Investigation, there to discuss Wachi's "secret communication activities in Mexico at the outbreak of the war."

Wachi was anything but placated; in fact, his frustration seemed to grow. Of course military attachés stationed overseas are involved in intelligence activities, he argued, but that didn't mean it was necessary to imprison him in a place like Sugamo just to investigate them. "I see no reason why you should do this to me," Wachi said.

The FBI agent did not argue. Wachi recalled that he actually apologized for holding him at Sugamo, but he had an investigation to conduct. "We suspect that you must have been in close contact with some very high ranking official in the US Military department," he told Wachi. "We have to know who your partner was." As he spoke, the agent offered Wachi a Lucky Strike cigarette, quite the luxury not only for a prisoner but for any Japanese under the American occupation. They lit their cigarettes and smoked together. Wachi felt himself calming down. "OK," he said. "I'll tell you anything I know."

Back home, Wachi's family struggled to get by without him. His imprisonment caused issues for his children at school and with playmates, who taunted the children about their father, the war criminal.

Chikako knew that her father hadn't done anything wrong, and she desperately clung to that faith as the weeks dragged on. Whatever he had done, she was sure he'd done it for the sake of the nation.

To help the family, fifteen-year-old Chikako found a job, even though it was unusual for girls to work at the time. With the help of her godmother, she managed to snag a position as a clerk at the American GHQ. She worked on the ninth floor of the tallest building she'd ever been in and was enamored with the view. She got free Coca-Cola.[29]

Two days before Christmas, 1946, Chikako's father gave an affidavit as a witness. This time, it was not about Wachi's operations in Mexico, but about events surrounding what became known as the Marco Polo Bridge Incident of July 7, 1937, not far from the city today called Beijing or from Japanese-controlled Manchuria, putting it squarely in contentious territory.[30] Confusion at a bridge crossing led to an exchange of gunfire between Japanese and Chinese forces. Although attempts were made in the aftermath to de-escalate tensions, neither side was willing to politically concede.

According to Wachi's sworn statement, while at his communications post in the Naval Radio Receiving Office in Owada, Saitama prefecture, where he was serving as lieutenant commander, Wachi intercepted an urgent telegram from a US naval officer in Peking on July 10. It said that members of China's 29th Army were not pleased with the agreement between Japan and China and were planning to attack Japanese forces.[31] Wachi "considered this telegram very important" and telephoned Japan's naval general staff office. But it was a Saturday afternoon, and nobody was there. He then called a commander at the Navy Ministry and relayed the message. Wachi testified that he later heard that the message was passed along once more, to the adjutant of the war ministry, but "at first the army did not believe it," he recalled, because it had happened on the same day that the negotiation agreement was proposed. How could they have decided so quickly?

The message was not taken seriously. The Marco Polo Bridge Incident would become the flashpoint as tensions between China and Japan escalated into widespread fighting across China, triggering the Sino-Japanese War and, in many ways, the Pacific Theater of the Second World War. The inaction over what Wachi perceived to be an important telegram would torment him until his dying days. During his time in prison, with nothing to do but "meditate and look back upon the past, I was keenly aware and repentant more than ever of the unfortunate decision we had to follow. I was particularly regretful about the urgent cable in the first episode. If it had been sent to General Kawabe, the China Incident must have been prevented so there had never been the World War II. I can't help recalling ruefully the judgment of the Army Adjutant General."

Wachi's testimony was just one piece of the Tokyo War Crimes Trial—proceedings that were met with irony by the Japanese public, many of whom were still trying to eke out a life among the decimated, firebombed remains of their homes, or knew victims of the atomic bombings. The courtroom testimony, of course, told of the horrors of Japanese atrocities across Asia, from Nanking to Manila and Burma and Bataan, not to mention the ultimate betrayal in the eyes of the court's largest figure, the United States: the attack on Pearl Harbor.

But it was a "political event," a "victors' justice," one that told half the story. Behind closed doors at the White House, even Henry Stimson, the former US secretary of war, had expressed his concerns to Truman: that America's firebombing tactics in Japan could earn the country "the reputation of outdoing Hitler in atrocities."[32] And that assessment did not even include the atomic bombings of Hiroshima and Nagasaki.

Along with the confusion created by the exclusion of Emperor Hirohito in the proceedings, the tarnished legacy of the Tokyo War Crimes Trial would feed into the subsequent struggle of Japan's reckoning with the war, which continues even today. "It is impossible to understand East Asia's tensions today without considering what is ominously referred to as the 'history issue' left from World War II," wrote Gary J. Bass in his seminal telling of the trial. "The spectacular proceedings of the Tokyo trial remain an obsession in Japanese, Chinese, and Korean politics, as well as in many of their neighbors."[33]

In November 1948, the remaining class A defendants (two had died during the trial) were found guilty. Seven were sentenced to death; others received sentences of up to life behind bars.[34] Just after midnight on December 23, two years after Wachi's witness statement, six generals—including Hideki Tojo—and a civilian were hanged in the middle of the night at Sugamo. No reporters or photographers were allowed to witness the execution.[35]

In the 1970s, the infamous prison was torn down. In its place rose one of the tallest skyscrapers in Asia at the time, called Sunshine 60.[36]

The curiosity of American intelligence officials would follow Wachi even after Sugamo was behind him. A report from April 1953, declassified and released by the CIA in 2006 as part of the

Nazi War Crimes Disclosure Act, described him: "Speaks good English, is a large man for a Japanese and is in extremely vigorous health. Has characteristics of a forceful leader."[37]

He returned home to Kichijoji, a neighborhood west of central Tokyo largely spared from the firebombing of the city during the war, and plunged into his new life as a Buddhist priest. He waited for approval to return to Iwo Jima. Under American control, the island was essentially a mass grave, with thousands of dead Japanese soldiers lying inside the vast underground network of tunnels from which they had defended the island. Their remains deserved better, and Wachi wanted to be the one who brought them home.

In January 1952, nearly seven years after the battle, his request was granted.[38] Though the authority granting permission was the Japanese Government Ministry of Foreign Affairs, certificate number 951 approving his visit was written in English, a sign of occupation times. (In April 1952, the American occupation of Japan would end. Power and territory were returned to the country, with the exception of several islands, including Iwo Jima, which remained under US control.[39]) The purpose of his visit, permitted from January 25 to February 29, 1952, was "holding a memorial service for the war deads [*sic*]." His occupation was noted as priest.

Returning to Iwo's black sand beaches, Wachi put up memorial statues and prayed for the departed souls "without distinction of nationality"—reciting Buddhist sutras from his knees and sharing a message "to the spirits of the dead of both countries."[40] He performed these rites in both English and Japanese.

He entered the caves, which had been severely damaged by flamethrowers and bombing raids. To his horror, the skulls of many of the deceased appeared to be missing. Numerous relics remained in the underground bunkers, but not as many as there should have been, Wachi knew. Many of those items must have made the trip across the Pacific to America.

He would need help getting them back home.

CHAPTER 8

SYRACUSE, NEW YORK / MARCH 1970

After visiting Tokyo and Hong Kong during the remainder of the 1970 reunion trip, Marty and Janet Connor returned home to Syracuse. For the first time in a long time, Marty considered his own souvenirs. They meant little to him now. Whatever need he'd felt after the war to keep the items, show them off, prove he'd been there, seemed to have melted away. He made up his mind and started with the pay records he'd taken from a dead Japanese soldier. They were official documents, likely to contain the name of the original owner.

On a plain white sheet of paper, he typed a letter dated March 24, 1970:

Dear Mr. Wachi:
I have enclosed items obtained by me while on Iwo Jima in February and March 1945.

All were found on the Northern end of Iwo Jima during the last days of fighting.

I sincerely hope they will bring comfort to the relatives and families of the deceased.

My wife and myself wish to thank you and the other members of your group, for the hospitality shown us during our visit to your country.

Very truly yours,
Martin C. Connor

Marty placed the letter and the fragile pay records in a brown envelope and wrote the monk's address on the front. He sent it from the post office, and then he waited.

Would Wachi find the owner? Was the bereaved family still alive? Would Marty even hear back from Wachi?

It had been twenty-five years since Marty had pocketed the souvenirs, objects he'd taken as mere trophies yet which, he now knew, held more importance.

Physical objects have been central to human life since the beginning—whether for wealth or practicality or sentimentality or some combination. What might be meaningless or worthless to someone is a treasure to another; this much has always been understood.

A group of researchers examined this phenomenon in *Tangible Things: Making History Through Objects*:

How do material things function in human use? Humans gather them, nurture them, walk across them, climb them, kill them, eat them, make them, wear them, tell stories about them, bury them, revere them, destroy them, claim descent from them, forbid them to one another, give them to one another, exchange them, and much more. By manipulating them, humans articulate their own relationships with one another. Various human societies perform all these actions—and more—differently from each other, often in mutually incomprehensible ways. In order to perform all these actions in a repeatable manner, humans distinguish things from one another, name them, and group them.

Yet, the writers continue, "things are radically unstable." They can morph and shape-shift, figuratively and literally, taking on new meanings over the course of the "life of a thing."[1]

In many ways, things are just like memory, which is fickle and fluid in its own right. Memory warps and congeals over time, taking new forms in a way that often self-preserves—a defense mechanism of sorts, against one's actions, words, or even thoughts of the past. "The historical self is created to keep dissonance at bay," journalist David Carr wrote in his 2008 memoir, "and render the subject palatable in the present. . . . People remember what they can live with more often than how they lived."[2]

For what is an object if not a thing, if not a memory in physical form?

The object, or a memory, can alter in the presence of something or someone else—a revision of the past, so as not to offend, depending on the company one finds oneself in. Objects can expose a new perspective based on what's around or not around, "revealing new aspects of themselves by virtue of being seen in unfamiliar surroundings."[3]

"Stories about objects often begin with a basic set of questions: What is it? Who made it? How did it get here? What is it worth? These questions produce narratives about provenance and value, the kinds of stories that dealers and collectors require and that viewers of the popular PBS television show *Antiques Roadshow* have come to expect," write the authors of *Tangible Things.* "Historians, on the other hand, usually reach for a bigger set of questions. For them, the focus is seldom on the objects themselves but on larger themes that objects might evoke or illustrate. As a consequence, in historical narratives, objects usually play at best a supporting role. The usual strategy is simply to acknowledge the existence of each object—as the first, the oldest, the most important, or the most telling example of whatever it is the narrator is trying to tell. Both of these approaches have value," they argue, because "when seemingly narrow queries about where things came from and how they got there are placed next to seemingly bigger questions, interesting things begin to happen. Sometimes the central characters in a story change. Sometimes entirely new stories begin to emerge."

A month after Marty sent the pay records to Wachi, a white envelope arrived in his mailbox. A single sheet of thin, trifold paper lay tucked inside. It was typed, with a smooth handwritten signature penned at the bottom, and dated April 29, 1970:

> *Dear Mr. Martin C. Connor,*
> *It took about three weeks to find out the proper bereaved family of the war-dead who was described in your letter dated March 31, 1970.*[4]

The family is living in a town named Takahara in Miyazaki Prefecture of Kyushu.

As the name and the native town of the war-dead were written in a deposit pass-book among the items which were enclosed in your letter, I could contact with the Town Office asking to find out the bereaved family and its address, and then I could deliver the items to them through the Town Office and also inform the circumstances when you had found them on the western side of Iwo Jima near the sulfur quarry about February 26, 1945.

According to the Town Office, the grandmother of the war-dead among the family is still alive with the age of one hundred and three years, who is the oldest person in the prefecture, and in delight and gratitude of the family were quite beyond description. Now they could not only recover those items, but also learn the true date and spot of the war-dead by your kind letter.

They are wishing to know as much as possible in detail the circumstances when you obtained the items from the war-dead. By the small pictures of yourself and your wife, I could recall you well, specially I remember well Mrs.'s face through the glass window at the Haneda Air Port when I saw you off in the last night.

Any how, the Reunion on Iwo Jima of this time was quite significant and I think, your letter shows its actual proof.

Yours very sincerely,

Tsunezo Wachi

President, Association of Iwo Jima.

Tsunezo Wachi's signature on a letter to Marty Connor, April 29, 1970 (photo: Samantha Bresnahan)

Marty was pleased to know he had helped these families in some small way. With a focused determination, he unearthed more souvenirs to send. He also began to spread the word among his veteran buddies. Maybe this could become a new mission, a humanitarian one. Maybe together they could try to heal, both for themselves and for these complete strangers, the families of their former enemy.

At the reunion on Iwo Jima, Wachi had invited the American veterans to join his Iwo Jima Association of Japan. Near the end of 1970, Marty took him up on the offer. In a letter dated December 24, 1970—Christmas Eve—Wachi confirmed Marty's membership:

> *Dear Mr. Martin C Connor:*
> *Please forgive the delay in acknowledging [to] you that we were in receipt of your membership card and the check for your initiation fee.*
>
> *Now that your membership card is in our file with those of other members of the US and people all over Japan, we*

wish our good will and effort will help console the souls of the
war-dead and promote peace in the world.

Thanking you for your joining our association.
Sincerely Yours,
Tsunezo Wachi
President, Association of Iwojima.

On September 15, 1972, Wachi typed another letter, this one to
Charles Early, the organizer of the 1970 reunion on Iwo Jima.
Wachi was writing in response to a letter he'd received from yet
another US Marine veteran of Iwo Jima, which had opened with
this line:

Years pass, people age, opinions and causes change and in that
thought I find myself as the Secretary of the North Dakota Iwo
Jima Veterans Association making an effort to communicate
with you and your group in Japan.

The veteran asked how his group could get to Iwo Jima.
Wachi thought that Charles, having spearheaded those complicated efforts two years before, would be able to offer advice. He
received Charles's reply swiftly.

Dear Wachi-san,
It was so good to hear from you again. I think of you often.
This last year I was President of the Fifth Marine Division
Association and we had our Convention in Sarasota. We
showed copies of the NBC movies taken on Iwo Jima and also

*the ones taken by General Jones of the Third Marine Division.
Needless to say you were quite prominent in them. . . . The
Marines and their families who went to Iwo Jima have come
to all three of our conventions since then in very high numbers.
We talk about our thrilling experience many, many times. All
agree it is one of the high points in their lives.*

May God be with you.
Very truly yours,
Charles E. Early

Only twenty-seven years before, had circumstances been
marginally different, had Wachi still been in command of Iwo
Jima on the nineteenth day of the second month of 1945, Wachi
and any one of these men—Charles Early, Marty Connor, the
Marine whose letter had prompted this correspondence, or even
NBC reporter John Rich, himself a veteran of the battle—would
have fought to the death. It could have been their families chained
to the unknown.

"Where and how did he die?"

Masataka Shiokawa knew what it felt like to search for
answers, and closure, and peace. He would ask himself that question over and over as he grew into adulthood, a piece of his soul
missing, a piece that had died with his father on Okinawa.[5] He
was desperate to know, but he was busy with work and unsure of
where to start based on the limited information he had ("Killed in
action. June 22, 1945. Komesu, Okinawa Island").

Another soldier in his father's regiment had provided a written record of the unit's last movements. The 36th, the soldier said,

had retreated to Mabuni in Itoman City in May 1945, but on the evening of June 22, the same date listed on Masamitsu Shiokawa's notice of death, the unit was ordered further north, near the top of Okinawa's main island, in the Kunigami area.

Those who remained in place survived, but those who moved north to follow orders were killed.

Shiokawa could merely speculate that perhaps his father had been one of the unlucky ones who'd headed north to Kunigami, only to meet his end some twenty-four hours or less before the battle was over.

Shiokawa had halfway given up on the idea of bringing his father home when he saw a newspaper headline in December 1976: "Recovering the Remains of Fellow Soldiers in Okinawa." The article profiled a man named Toshihide Takada, an employee of the Japanese National Railways at Kagoshima Station. He had fought at Okinawa and now was trying to recover the remains of the men left behind. "With renewed hope," Shiokawa later wrote in his memoir, "I immediately contacted Mr. Takada and met with him. When I showed him the military postcard that my father had sent to my mother, he shouted out, 'I was in the same unit!'"

The 36th Regiment, however, had contained some two thousand men. Masamitsu Shiokawa had been in the 116th wireless platoon, and Takada had been assigned to wired communications. He had not known Masamitsu, but the coincidence was striking. Takada shared his experiences with Masataka, by then thirty-two years old—just one year older than the age of his father at his death.

Takada had gone to Okinawa shortly after it was returned by the Americans to Japan. He had visited the bunker where he'd hidden during the battle, he told Shiokawa, and found the remains of his fellow soldiers "abandoned, just the way he remembered from back then." Takada was stunned—after all this time, he thought the men would have been recovered and returned home to a proper resting place. This "postwar reality," he said, shocked him and made him feel guilty. Motivated by that guilt, he began efforts to recover the bodies.

Yet there was only so much Takada could do as one individual, a predicament Shiokawa had become all too familiar with. Takada requested help from both local and national governments, only to be told by the Japanese authorities that "the recovery of remains in Okinawa has been completed."

Shiokawa empathized with Takada's frustration. "Where and how did he die?" continued to echo in his mind, coupled with the knowledge that the bodies of so many men remained right where they had died. Conceivably, so did his father's. He had no memories of his father; he had been too young when his father left. Shiokawa got to know him only through a few photos on the family altar and the small, tan, handwritten postcards sent from the front lines, their ink fading ever so slowly, as if symbolizing that the time to find Masamitsu would someday run out. As if he would be erased from his son's life forever. As if he had never existed in the first place.

In February 1977, Shiokawa made his first trip to Okinawa, alongside Takada, and saw scenes that remain "burned" into his mind: "I have a vivid memory of the first time I entered a natural bunker near the Mabuni Beach in Itoman City. As soon as I stepped inside, I saw skeletal remains, with hand grenades and other weapons and artifacts lying nearby. It looked as though they had just been scattered around recently. 'This can't be. . . .' I could not believe what I was seeing."

Finding his father seemed an impossible task in a skeleton graveyard, if not for one clue provided by Shiokawa's mother before she died. Masamitsu carried a personal seal into battle, she told him, made of buffalo horn. And though the bodies had been reduced to bones, perhaps Shiokawa could find that horn, and with it the resting place of his father. Perhaps he could finally bring him home.

The gama (caves) were eerie and quiet, the thick rock walls dulling almost all sound from the outside. Some were large, interconnected through a series of man-made tunnels. Others were tiny, barely big enough for one man, created naturally in the rock formations dotting the hillsides. Shielded from Okinawa's subtropical climate, many of the gama and their contents had remained untouched since the day the Japanese commander

Masamitsu Shiokawa's name enshrined on the memorial wall at Okinawa, which bears the names of all killed in the battle, regardless of nationality (photo: Samantha Bresnahan)

of the Okinawa forces refused surrender, choosing—or feeling forced—to die by suicide instead.

Some skeletons remained propped where they fell, a bullet hole visible in the helmet and in the skull. Others were only partially intact, arm or leg bones missing, perhaps from injury or simply lost over time. Unexploded grenades sat next to their owners' remains. Bits of metal from gas masks and uniforms lay preserved and protected from rain and wind, the caves having provided a natural time capsule.

Shiokawa scooped up a bit of stone from Komesu, where his father had died, to take home and place at the family altar next to the "soul stone" he and his mother had received from the government. But it was not enough; it would never be enough. His father deserved to come home.

Shiokawa's mind told him it was impossible to find his father, but his heart pleaded otherwise. He'd have to try.

Roughly four hundred thousand Americans died in the European and Pacific Theaters of World War II; today, more than seventy-one thousand remain missing in Europe and the Pacific.[6] A robust effort is under way to identify and return missing Americans from the Second World War, the Korean War, the Cold War, and the Vietnam War. The Defense Department estimates that nearly thirty-nine thousand of the total missing can be recovered.[7]

Out of a nation of 77 million, about 2.4 million military personnel—mostly young men—died across Asia in the name of Japan's imperial government during the Second World War. Nearly eight decades later, more than 1 million are still missing.[8]

Half of Japan's war dead have not, and likely will not, ever return home. When Shiokawa began his efforts in the late 1970s, he could not foresee that this would still be the case more than forty years later. If he had—well, that does something to a person's psyche.

There were flashes of promise over the years, enough to fan Shiokawa's eternal flame of hope. Seven years after the end of the war, the Japanese government began an official effort to recover the remains of the 2.4 million lost souls.[9] On June 16, 1952, the Lower House of the National Diet of Japan passed a resolution devoted to the "collection and repatriation of the remains of the war dead overseas." It was a herculean task, to be sure. Millions of the dead were scattered across a region where Japan was most certainly not welcome.

The first recovery effort took place over five years, in locations ranging from Okinawa to Saipan, Guam, the Philippines, and beyond—yet yielded only 12,000 sets of remains.[10] A decade would pass before another recovery team tried again, from 1967 to 1972, resulting in the collection of 115,000 sets. A final effort brought back another 100,000 by 1975.

What to do with the remains was another issue altogether, as many could not be identified. Chidorigafuchi National Cemetery, located in central Tokyo, opened on March 28, 1959, as a home to Japan's unknown war dead, similar to the Tomb of the Unknown Soldier in Arlington, Virginia.[11] Yet even Chidorigafuchi, intended as a secular place of rest—as distinct from the controversial Yasukuni Shrine located down the road—received criticism for glossing over events that led to the need for the national cemetery in the first place.[12]

While in Okinawa, Shiokawa saw personal effects littered throughout the gama. Resentment toward the enemy gripped his chest. He looked at the artifacts around him and thought about his own father. How could he rest peacefully in a place like this? Shiokawa imagined the other families just like him who were searching endlessly for answers: When and how did their loved ones die, and where? He felt the Japanese government had failed to provide that information to the countless families who'd been left behind.

There were so many things Shiokawa could not do. He could not change the past. He could not alter the outcome of defeat. He could not save his father. But the son of a young man killed at war could become a crusader of peace for the living and the dead.

CHAPTER 9

On May 30, 1984, Tsunezo Wachi sat down at the typewriter to respond to a letter from Marty Connor in which Marty had inquired about the status of Wachi's work. "A former marine who was on Iwo Jima with me in 1945 has given me a diary and some personal pictures that he obtained from the body of a Japanese soldier who was killed by shell fire," Marty had written. "I would be happy to send these to you if you are still locating bereaved families of those who fought on Iwo Jima."[1]

Wachi was still very much involved, despite approaching his eighty-fourth birthday.

Dear Mr. Connor,
This acknowledges the receipt of your letter dated March 23
and I have to apologize for my rudeness in responding so late.

Be that as it may, we have much interesting of your kind letter and we do hope to send us those items which you have with a memo of your comrade concerning the date and location when he got them if possible.

We may be able to find out the proper bereaved family of those items using the net work of branches of our association all over Japan.

Waiting those items from you.

Yours very truly,

Tsunezo Wachi

This time, it was Marty's turn to delay the response. His curiosity over what the personal diary of a Japanese soldier on Iwo Jima might have said overshadowed any urgency in returning it. Ultimately true to his word, however, he packed it up and sent it to Wachi on November 29.

Dear Tsunezo Wachi,

I am sorry for the delay in sending the enclosed diary; I was interested in having it translated, but couldn't find anyone to do it for me.

I pray you will be successful in locating the bereaved family of the deceased. Please inform them that the diary, manual and pictures were in the soldier's uniform pocket. The items were found on his body as we advanced up the western side of Iwo Jima just past Hill 262. Near Nishi Village.

The soldier was apparently moving forward with other comrades, when a heavy barrage of artillery caught them unprotected and many were suddenly killed. We saw, perhaps, twenty bodies in the area when we passed through after the artillery lifted.

Tsunezo, please let the family know that the Marines who fought on Iwo Jima had the greatest respect for the Japanese soldiers and Navy Personnel who fought against them.

I appreciate hearing from you again, and hope you can locate the soldier's family.

Sincerely,

Martin C. Connor

The careful phrasing, devoid of gruesome detail, and even the use of passive language had become customary for Marty when he talked about the war. It was almost as though he was sparing those on the other end, especially now that Marty felt he had a connection to them.

The details of the battle, of death, were ones he would not have wanted his own family to know, and so he buffed the edges, made the information that much easier to bear. Perhaps he subconsciously did so as much for his own benefit as for the Japanese families, and even for Wachi, whom Marty respected greatly.

Yet it wasn't customary to loot the body of a soldier you weren't responsible for killing. When asked decades later if it was really naval gunfire that had killed the man, Marty stuck to the same version of events: artillery on the western side of the island.[2]

Not long before Christmas, a letter arrived in Marty's mailbox, bearing the familiar typeface of Wachi's typewriter.

Dear Martin C. Connor,

This acknowledges the receipt of your letter dated Nov. 29 and those items which you got on Iwojima.

It did not take much time to fined [sic] out the proper bereaved family of the war dead. The name, written in the diary, is SAKUICHI HURUSHOO, an army soldier belonged to the 314 Battalion. His widow named MASUE HURUSHOO is living at FUKUOKA City in KYUSHUU and a member of our Association. So it was very easy to contact with her.

According to a report of a committee of the KYUSHUU branch, she was very pleased to hear this news and eagerly to get those items.

I will send those items to the committee to deliver them to her and also ask him to send me pictures of the delivery.

I have meetings with the representatives of Iwojima Return Committee this Thursday and Friday to confer about reunion on Iwojima on 19 Feb. 1985. I heared [sic] that 200 Americans including veterans and bereaved families will come to Tokyo and Iwojima. I will introduce this instance to them and ask them to urge the same thing to the veterans at that time. Anyhow, your items came to me indeed in good time.

Yours sincerely,

Tsunezo Wachi

President, Association of Iwojima.

If you had opened the *Boston Globe* to page 2 on Friday, February 15, 1985, you would have seen many things. Thursday's Massachusetts lottery number was 2143, and if you matched all four numbers in that order, your payout was $1,720. A correction fixed a percentage about Korean elections reported the previous day. As catalogued in the Index, the Sports section, beginning on page 49, promised stories about a Celtics victory over Seattle and a Bruins tie with the Kings. The International section had details on remains found in Laos, believed to be those of US troops missing in action (page 3). In South Africa, Nelson Mandela must accept terms or remain jailed (page 8).

But page 2 was dominated by one story and a corresponding photo. A pull quote at the top, in bold letters, read, "Iwo Jima is my temple." It was attributed to Tsunezo Wachi. The Centerpiece feature of that day's paper sat under the headline "Former Commander Now Devotes His Life to Praying for Dead Victims of Battle." A tall black-and-white portrait of Wachi filled the right side of the page. His eyebrows remained bushy, but his face showed his years, the bags under his eyes, the wrinkles on his thin neck. The article's dateline was Tokyo, and reporter Tom Ashbrook's opening sentences wasted no time in getting to the core of the story about the naval officer turned priest: "Tsunezo Wachi didn't die in the battle of Iwo Jima, but even now, at age 84, there are days when he wishes that he could have. Almost every day."

The story described "the walls of Wachi's modest home in suburban Tokyo," which were plastered in Iwo Jima imagery: photographs, paintings, sketches. Ashbrook wrote that Wachi, "intelligent" and "clear-thinking," was quick to tell him, a stranger, that he had seen "ghosts of the war dead on Iwo Jima, walking in bloody, torn uniforms and kamikaze headbands," specters that Wachi had called after, "begging them to come home to Japan."

Wachi had argued that particular point with some, including a Japanese survivor of the battle named Satoru Ōmagari. In a rare interview, Ōmagari, who had left Wachi's association in the 1970s over the dispute, told historian Dan King, "Iwo Jima is part of Japan, it is not a foreign country. We defenders said if we died we would become the soil of Iwo Jima."[3]

It was not a position Wachi would compromise on. The barren island was not their homeland, nor could their families visit, and so it would never be a proper resting place. It seems Wachi never could absolve his guilt over Iwo Jima and its war dead, what the *Globe* story called "the one and only focus of his Buddhist devotions."

"Even now," Wachi told Ashbrook, "I want to live alone on the island. Always on the island, alone."

The story was published just days before the fortieth anniversary of the battle's beginnings, for which another reunion was planned, and over which Wachi would once again preside in prayer as a member of the Japanese delegation. As part of the ceremony, two assistants will blow into conch shells, Wachi said, calling out to the spirits of the war dead—both Japanese and American.

"Their only differences were of tradition," the priest told the reporter. "As human beings, they were the same."

Four years later, in late 1989, Wachi lay in a hospital bed. He was being treated for heart and lung trouble, ailments that had followed him ever since one of the pre-Iwo bombing raids had blasted him from his post.[4] Despite the setting and the fact his eighty-nine-year-old body needed rest, Wachi continued making phone calls and facilitating returns. The work could never stop.

Tsunezo Wachi and his wife, Toshiko (courtesy Rosa Chikako Ogawa)

But it was not Wachi's funeral that his children would need to plan first. On a cold morning, Wachi's dear wife, Toshiko, suddenly passed away. Chikako's brother visited their father in the hospital to tell him the news. "Oh," Wachi said calmly, "she went ahead of me."

In that case, there was one thing left to do. Wachi called upon an old friend, a Spanish Jesuit. There in the hospital, he was baptized, taking the name Peter. While in prison all those decades before, during the Tokyo War Crimes Trial, Wachi—believing Buddhism too intricate and difficult for women to learn—had instructed his wife to devote the rest of the family to Catholicism, which she gladly did, having studied at a Christian college. She and the children were baptized in 1947, when Chikako took the name Rosa.[5] Now, on his deathbed forty years later, Wachi could join them at last.

Rosa visited him in the hospital on a day when snow fell from the sky, just as it had on the day of her mother's funeral. Wachi gazed out the window from his bed.

"Why don't you go home," he said softly to his daughter. "Your children are waiting for you."

"Okay, Dad," Rosa replied. "I'll come back again."

She wondered how many more opportunities she'd have to see him, this man who was larger than life for so many, who had dedicated himself to a cause he'd held dear, a cause that had consumed his every moment. He was all those things to be sure, a looming figure in Japanese history, and he was also her father, frail and ill, in a hospital bed. A father she loved and respected.

The next morning, Rosa received a call from the hospital.[6] Nineteen days after his wife's passing, Peter Tsunezo Wachi died on February 2, 1990, and with him, Marty Connor's main connection to Japan.

It would take another fourteen years and a crumpled flag found in a shed in western New York before that channel would reopen.

MARIETTA, GEORGIA / APRIL 2021

When I imagined history's arrival on my doorstep, I did not picture a recycled food-delivery box. It showed up shortly after six o'clock on a sunny Monday evening, held together by thick layers of packing tape. Each strip ran atop a fading "Freshly" logo. It had been dropped off with little fanfare, despite what I knew was inside.

My heart rate increased as I picked up our cheap green and gray box cutter to carefully slice through the tape, praying that

I didn't catch any interior contents on the blade. From behind a small wooden gate that separates our kitchen from the foyer, our golden retriever puppy watched my every move. I heard my husband typing in the office upstairs. I had told him I'd wait for him before opening it, but I couldn't help myself.

I folded back the top flaps and let out a deep breath. I wondered if this is how Marty Connor felt, the man at the center of this story, every time a box arrived at his door, as they often did over the course of nearly half a century. History had shown up at my house, but it was merely a layover for the box before it traveled much farther, back to where it belonged.

Inside the box, placed at the very top in a sealed plastic bag, was a pair of soft, olive-green pants, almost startling in their simplicity. Beneath them, two handwritten postcards were tucked into a white envelope, the ink of the Japanese characters fading to the point of near invisibility. Also inside the envelope, postmarked from New Orleans, a letter written in cursive on graph paper read, "Enclosed are two postcards my father, Joseph A. Bernard, 2nd Division, USMC, picked up on Guadalcanal 1942."

I held these pieces of history in my hands and felt a range of emotions: surprise, awe, gratitude. Sadness. Responsibility.

This journey had begun eleven years earlier, in 2010, when I'd first learned of a man named Marty Connor, a US Marine veteran of Iwo Jima who was sending stolen relics of World War II back to the families of the Japanese soldiers whose bodies they'd been taken from. The contents of the box, until recently, had been stored in his home office in Syracuse. The letter from New Orleans was addressed to him. But he had died the preceding December at age ninety-four, before he could finish the last part of his mission.

What I knew of the war had come from the history books of my western Pennsylvania high school and my local library, and from a desire to learn and read as much as I could about the Holocaust. My curiosity was driven largely by a close family friend, who, when I was a child, refused to wear short sleeves because they would expose the tattooed numbers on his forearm, inciting questions he was not willing to answer. It was also driven by my father's genealogy research, which had recently unearthed relatives with a cause of death listed as "Nazi Camp Auschwitz" and "Nazi Camp Sobibor."

Then there was my maternal grandfather's connection to the war. On December 7, 1941, he was on board the USS *Maryland*, which was docked at Pearl Harbor. He survived the battle, and our proximity to that slice of American history became pinned like a badge of honor on my whole family. My grandfather, who did not openly speak of his war experiences until much later in his life, did have one public display—a bumper sticker on his car, fading and peeling, but the words still legible: *Pearl Harbor survivor*. People used to tuck little notes behind his windshield wiper: "Glad you survived." "Thank you for your service." I learned to be proud of it, too. And so my frame of reference for the Pacific Theater was Japan's initial act of war against the United States, as it was for many other American families, Marty's included.

The name on the box's return address label read "Terry Connor," one of Marty's sons. *Could you help*, Terry had asked me several weeks before. "I think that's important to get [the uniform pants and postcards] back to Japan," he texted me. "It's what dad would want."

Terry had placed in the box all his father's Iwo Jima–related files—including Marty's original letters home to his parents during the battle—and anything else he could find about the forty-plus years Marty spent returning items taken from Pacific battlefields, starting with his own and then those from veterans and their descendants all over the United States.

Having been told that the box would also contain old tapes, I was prepared with a cassette player I'd ordered in anticipation of this moment, itself a relic of times past. I slid in a tape and hit play. Marty's raspy voice echoed through the headphones. It was a story I'd heard him recount dozens of times. Yet hearing him again gave me a renewed sense of appreciation and perspective.

I recalled visiting Marty in 2016 while conducting research for this book. I'd first interviewed him six years earlier for a documentary on CNN International. His home, sided with gray wooden slats, sat on fifty acres of land, on which he had planted, by his own count, some eighteen thousand trees, most of them pine.[7] From there, he could see no other houses.

On that land, Marty had raised a family, excelled in his career, experienced unbelievable joys, and weathered devastating heartbreaks. And he had also found purpose far beyond that house on the hill.

I sat in my rental car in his driveway. Through the closed car window, I could hear the *ping-ping-ping* of the halyard against the flagpole that proudly flew both American and Marine Corps flags. Before our first meeting, in December 2010, he had gotten up at five in the morning to clear the driveway of knee-deep snow for our production crew. He was eighty-four years old.

I walked toward the house. A gold sign hanging above the doorbell read, "House of Connor. Established Oct. 26, 1967."

Before I could knock, he appeared, opening the front screen door with a warm smile. Wearing a cotton shirt and khaki cargo shorts over his thin frame, he looked and sounded exactly as I remembered. I hadn't kept in touch with him as much as I'd wanted to, but it was as if we'd last seen each other six weeks before, not six years.

Marty and I wandered into the kitchen, where he offered me a drink. I accepted the glass of water gratefully; it was unseasonably warm for Central New York, and the air hung heavy with a humidity not often associated with that part of the country. Our only defense against the heat was a small, black oscillating fan perched at the other end of the room. Despite the temperature, Marty poured himself a steaming cup of tea.

At the kitchen table, marked by years of use with indentations in the wood, Marty carefully opened the top flap of an overstuffed file folder. One by one, he removed pieces of his past. There were old letters, scans of magazine articles, a photocopied list of Iwo Jima casualties. And there were handwritten personal checks made out to him, pinned to some of the letters with paperclips. The dates on the checks spanned decades.

I looked up at Marty. "You never cashed these?"

He traced the edge of a check. "It was never about that," he said quietly. "I told people they didn't have to send money, but they wanted to."

Marty didn't have to send what he did, either, but he wanted to.

We relocated to the seating area off the kitchen. Again, just as I remembered it. A small television faced a well-worn maroon recliner, the leather on the headrest peeling and faded. A framed print of Jesus watched over the room from the side table. Marty sat down in a wooden chair with his tea, offering me the recliner.

Above my head, a poster dwarfed the family photos on the wall. It was a map of Iwo Jima. Light blue represented the sea, white the island, and a flurry of red dots indicated the beaches upon which seventy thousand Marines, including the man sitting across from me, had descended on a February morning in 1945.

Many of those men chose to forget. But Marty kept the poster prominently displayed in his living room. He had for many years. He couldn't forget what he'd seen or what he'd done, so he didn't try. The memories still returned to him at night as he lay in bed, through dreams that were nightmares, or even during the daylight, as he sat in his living room.

He sipped from his mug and looked pointedly down at my green notebook, the empty white pages eager to absorb whatever he was willing to share with me.

"Where do you want to start?"

PART 2

CHAPTER 10

Shannon Moore had doubts.

She didn't know if returning the flag that her father, Arthur Pim, had taken from battle in the Philippines was such a good idea. Is that what her dad would have wanted?

"Your father was a kind man," her mother said. "I think he would be okay with this."[1] From what she remembered of her father during her childhood, Shannon agreed. But she only knew Arthur the father, not Arthur the soldier. What if she was making a big mistake? What if this was a wound that time could not heal, if feelings of resentment or hatred did not diminish, but instead festered or worsened?

Shannon's uncle Paul, her mother's younger brother and a drinking buddy of her father's, had fought in Vietnam and, having been exposed to Agent Orange, experienced his own personal hell. Regarding the flag, Paul told her, "You don't know what your father went through to get that." To her list of worries, Shannon added a fear of disrespecting her dad. Paul was a veteran, and Shannon valued his opinion. She could not criticize him for feeling that way; she didn't know what he'd been through.

She spoke to another uncle. Jack had fought at Okinawa during World War II, and while he did not outright say he disagreed with the idea of returning the flag, he told Shannon about watching Japanese women and children jumping from cliffs because the government had told them the Americans were coming to rape and kill them. He could still see the faces of kamikaze pilots targeting American troops. Jack's experience was more similar to what her father would have dealt with, how he might have felt.

Shannon's doubt worsened.

There was one more person to consult who would probably understand her father's perspective better than most. Shannon picked up the phone and dialed the house on the hill. Marty Connor's gravelly voice answered. She told him she was having second thoughts. *What if this isn't what my father intended for the flag?*

"Oh, your father knows what you're doing," Marty told her.

Shannon smiled. It was all she needed to hear. A sense of calm and peace instantly settled over her. She thanked Marty and resolved to go through with her original plan, her doubt eased if not erased. She believed she had been the one to find the flag for a reason; had it been anyone else, it would have ended up in the trash, regarded merely as a crumpled rag.

As she hung up the phone, it occurred to her that Marty and her father were around the same age. *This is what it would be like if he were still alive*, she thought. She felt as if, on some level, she'd just had the chance to speak with her dad. Marty had given her an unintended gift by answering the phone that day.

The gift would be returned, though Shannon didn't know it at the time. She was about to help Marty too. In the course of their initial research into the flag, Professor Mitsuaki Shimojo of the University at Buffalo had found a man in Japan who had recently started an organization to help Americans return belongings to the Japanese families of the war dead.[2] It seemed the man had lost his father during the Battle of Okinawa, giving him a personal connection to the work. His name was Masataka Shiokawa.

The sun shone, a rare spring gift in Central New York, and it warmed Shannon as she and her family drove east over I-90 from Buffalo to Syracuse. The flag she had found among her father's possessions, inked with the name Jinichi Kodama, rested in a red frame, protected by glass. Today, April 29, 2004, it would take the next critical step in returning to where it belonged.

Shannon was anxious. Marty Connor was coming, along with three of his veteran buddies.[3] Masataka Shiokawa would be there, too, having traveled all the way from Japan. She would get to make the handoff in person and to meet and thank both Shiokawa and Marty, which felt important to her, because this had become about so much more than the flag.

Over the last year, Shannon's entire perspective on the Second World War—and her father's experiences in it—had changed. Along with her research into the Japanese flags and how to return them, she had learned more about the war itself. "I'm so much more aware of human suffering now, especially during wartime, and the families that are left behind," she told Japan's public media outlet Nippon Hōsō Kyōkai (NHK) for a documentary. "I have to shamefully admit, I never gave much thought to my father's military background," she added. "This has been a real eye-opening experience to know what he has gone through, what he lived with, and the decisions he had to make."[4]

Now it was time for Shannon's decision to pay off. Tom pulled the car up to the Best Western hotel near the Syracuse airport, and Shannon, Tom, and their daughter Sarah piled out. They walked inside, carrying the flag in its frame.

Earlier, as her resolve had wavered, Shannon had sat in her den at the computer. An overwhelming fragrance filled her senses. It was Old Spice, she realized. There was only one person in her life who ever wore Old Spice. She wasn't sure if she was the kind of person who believed in signs, but she couldn't ignore this one. A sense of peace settled over her. *My dad is okay with this*, she thought. *He's here with me.*

Masataka Shiokawa was going to America, and it was complicated. He had never been. He was not sure what to think, but he knew how he felt: defensive. He didn't want to feel that way; it just could not be helped. His mind told him he was about to stand face to face with the enemy. *These are people who killed Japanese*, he thought, the people who had killed his father in Okinawa—not directly, but still the thought remained.

Shiokawa traveled by himself, and though it was his first visit to the country, he was not going anywhere typically mentioned at the top of a guidebook, like New York City or Los Angeles or Washington, DC. But he was not there to sightsee. He was traveling to Syracuse, in Upstate or Central New York, depending on whom you asked. Shiokawa was going to meet Marty Connor and Shannon Moore.

Five years before, in 1999, Shiokawa had had a revelation. Two decades of focusing on recovering human remains had shown him something else: it wasn't just the bodies, or what was left of them, that had stayed behind. There were personal effects too. In lieu of bones, they provided a different sort of connection to the dead: something that had once belonged to them. In light of the fact that the human remains of the fallen were proving difficult to recover, perhaps there was a silver lining to the macabre practice of looting the dead. Shiokawa realized that thousands, if not tens of thousands, of Japanese soldiers' belongings must exist in America.

Much like the Kodama flag Shannon had found, the flag that kicked off Shiokawa's efforts had also come from Leyte, in the Philippines. In 1999, a Japanese woman in the United States reached out to Shiokawa after hearing of his recovery efforts.[5] A coworker had given her a flag, she said, and they would like to return it to the owner. Was that possible? A photo was enclosed with the letter, the writing visible on the silk fabric: "Masao Nagasaka, we are praying for your long-lasting fortune in battle."

Shiokawa considered the name: Masao Nagasaka, the name of the soldier who had carried the flag in battle. To find the relatives of one man, out of more than two million dead? The task felt daunting, but Shiokawa was determined. He inspected the photo of the flag more closely and saw another name: Nogata National School. "Could it be Nogata City in Fukuoka Prefecture, located next to Saga Prefecture where I live?" Shiokawa would later write. "I immediately went to the Nogata City Hall and showed them a copy of the flag."

The chairman of the prefecture's association of war-bereaved families said yes, and in fact, Nagasaka's sister-in-law was still alive—he knew her personally. Together, the chairman and Shiokawa visited her at home and showed her the photograph of the flag. She wanted it returned. The following May, the American who had the flag and his Japanese coworker journeyed to Japan and hand-delivered the flag to Nagasaka's tearful and grateful sister-in-law.

"I am going to tell my husband at the altar that his little brother is finally home," Shiokawa remembered her saying. He felt "profound happiness," and also a feeling of relief that the return had been successful.

He couldn't help himself—Shiokawa cried too.

The American who'd had possession of Nagasaka's flag lived in Kentucky. He asked neighbors and friends and coworkers about items taken from fallen Japanese soldiers that they might have, and suddenly there were more objects to return. Shiokawa thought, *There must be so many artifacts in America since they simply asked their neighbors and could get all these.* It was a breakthrough.

In 2002, Shiokawa founded a nonprofit organization, the NPO Incorporated Association for War Dead Memorial and Peace, to continue efforts to recover and return both human remains and personal artifacts. The group launched a bilingual website to assist both Americans and Japanese; it included photographs of objects waiting to return home.

Within four years, the association received some twelve hundred artifacts. Beyond the flags, there were swords and photographs and senninbari, each with a story to tell. The work was slow and arduous—few returns happened as quickly as the Nagasaka flag, if at all—turning Shiokawa and his small team into detectives of sorts, searching for and deciphering endless clues. Meanwhile, Shiokawa continued to work full-time at an insurance firm.

The flags were marked by brushstrokes that reflected a broader history of Asia. While the exact chronology remains uncertain, kanji—Japanese for "Chinese character"—likely arrived via a Korean man toting Chinese texts in the late fourth or early fifth century.[6] Historians believe that prior to that, Japan had no formal written language. By the seventh century, largely thanks to an exchange of scholars with China, including Japanese Buddhist monks, the kanji system had spread, eventually becoming the official written form of the Japanese language. And as they did with so much, the Japanese elevated calligraphy to an art form known as shodō.[7]

Writing styles were differentiated as block, cursive, or somewhere in between, with the meanings of characters derived from the order of the brushstrokes as well as from the strokes themselves. The meaning of some kanji on the flags was lost to time, either too faded and too hard to read or containing slight variations in brushstrokes that could make all the difference between the right name and the wrong one, a helpful clue or a misleading interpretation.

Sometimes the clue was the flag itself. "These flags don't usually have a lining like this," Shiokawa told members of a Japanese family in 2004, as he tried to find the surviving relatives of a soldier named Yoshio Kato. Unfortunately, more than one man with that name had died during the war. The flag in question had a thick lining. "This person may have been in a place with a cold climate," Shiokawa said. "They sometimes wrapped themselves in these flags to stay warm." But no one, not even the neighbors who came by to see the flag, recognized any signatures on it as belonging to anyone from that area. It was a dead end. This would happen more frequently than Shiokawa would have preferred. But he remained undeterred.

Over the next ten years, Shiokawa and his NPO would return more than 130 items, most often to surviving family members—rarely to the original owners themselves—across all forty-seven prefectures. These efforts meant that dozens of families finally knew what had happened to their loved ones. They had a way to remember them and to pray for them at the family altar, next to their other ancestors.

"I never had a chance to be a good son to my father. That's the truth," Shiokawa told a documentary crew in 2004, surrounded by Masamitsu's aging war postcards. "So now, I recover the remains and return the artifacts, because I think my father would be happy to see me do that. It is part of my being a good son to him. If there is an afterlife, I think he is surrounded by his war buddies, and he can tell them that his son is doing good."

In a dark gray suit with a white shirt and mustard tie, Shiokawa tried to calm his nerves. Shannon did the same. In the hallway of the hotel's first floor, beyond the breakfast area, they came face to face for the first time.

"Mr. Shiokawa?" Shannon asked tentatively. "Very nice to meet you." Shiokawa presented her with his business card, bowing his head slightly a few times.

"I gotta give you a hug!" Shannon said, unable to help herself, and her warmth caught Shiokawa off guard. He quickly recovered and returned her embrace. "Thank you for what you do," Shannon told him. "You do wonderful things."

Her husband, Tom, eased the bubble wrap away from the framed flag as Shiokawa watched patiently, a small smile on his face. They placed the flag on a wooden easel in one of the hotel's meeting rooms, the red frame and the circle of the Hinomaru striking against the stark white walls. Shiokawa picked up his digital camera and instructed Shannon and her daughter Sarah to pose next to the flag so he could capture the moment. If he could find the family, this was a photo he'd love to share with them.

"This is the best day ever," he said.

Before long, Marty arrived, along with three other Iwo Jima Marine veterans. In a navy-blue suit and tie, Marty introduced himself to Shiokawa. The pair shook hands, warm but businesslike. Shiokawa presented his business card.

Roughly twenty items from Syracuse and beyond were being handed over to Shiokawa that day, all to make the long trip home to Japan. Shannon watched as the older men examined the different objects.

"I think it's time for forgiveness," said Ray Salvie, one of Marty's veteran buddies. By then seventy-eight years old, Ray had also served in the Marines, as a mortarman. He had fought on Iwo Jima for twenty-four days.[8] He presented Shiokawa with a Japanese postcard taken from the battlefield. "Sixty years is a long time," Ray added, "and you can't hold a grudge."

There were others in the room, too, including Sean Kirst, the reporter with the Syracuse *Post-Standard* who had connected Marty and Shannon, and Professor Shimojo, on hand to translate, just as he had the year before, at the university in Buffalo. There was also a woman named Tomoko Stultz.

Tomoko lived a few houses down from Sean Kirst. Born in 1963 roughly one hundred miles north of Tokyo in Tochigi prefecture, Tomoko was raised and educated in Japan.[9] The war was not a topic covered widely in her schools. She doubted that she had ever met a Japanese veteran of the war—though it was more likely, she later realized, that she had, but they never mentioned it.

Although Hiroshima and Nagasaki were well-known, the stories she heard most often about Americans and the war were

From left: US Marine veterans Bob Cudworth, Ray Salvie, Nick Zingaro, and Marty Connor (courtesy Shannon Moore)

about chewing gum. During the occupation of Japan, American GIs passed out chewing gum and chocolate bars to young kids on the street. The kids were so enamored of the rare sweets that they learned to say, "Give me chewing gum" in English. By the time of Tomoko's childhood, the narrative of America and Japan was not one of bitter war but of prosperous rebuilding.

Eventually she met an American man while working in a language school in Tokyo. They married and decided in 1998 to relocate to his hometown of Syracuse. Tomoko began work as a teaching assistant in the city's school system, striking up friendships with her neighbors—including Sean Kirst. So of course he thought of her immediately when he found out a man named Shiokawa was coming all the way from Tokyo. *Do you want to meet this guy?* he'd asked her. *There will be Japanese flags.*

Japanese flags? Tomoko had not heard any of these war stories, but her curiosity won out. She wasn't quite sure what to expect, but once she saw what was happening, she immediately understood. And no history book could have ever provided an education quite as important as this one. The events of that day blew her away. Four old, gray-haired Marines were returning artifacts from battle to a Japanese man, the son of a soldier killed during the war. They could not directly communicate with each other, but they didn't need to. The emotions were written plainly on their faces.

Sean Kirst smiled. These salty old Marines, and this son of their former enemy, were getting along famously. It was a bit awkward at first, but they'd settled in. As he hoped might happen, Tomoko stepped in to help translate.

Marty Connor had a piece of yellow cloth, embroidered with flowers, that someone had sent him, pilfered from the pocket of a dead Japanese soldier during the fight for Okinawa, the same battle that had killed Shiokawa's father. The cloth was signed "T. Arakaki."

A translator interpreted the writing on the fabric. For all the years the scrap of cloth had been in the United States, from 1945 to 2004, it's likely that no one had ever known what it said. As they read out loud, goosebumps rose on Sean's arms.

Marty Connor hands over a flag and a yellow cloth to Masataka Shiokawa, in the dark gray suit (courtesy Shannon Moore).

Behind the shadow of the mountain,
in the river bed,
the precious blood is scattered.
And in the blood, flowers bloom,
with a wonderful fragrance.

Sean blinked back tears; Shiokawa openly cried.

The words hovered in the room long after they were spoken.

Shannon watched Marty present item after item to Shiokawa. There were photos, a helmet, more flags, and a blood-stained shirt. It suddenly all felt very real, that humans were capable of hurting each other in such ways. But Marty and Shiokawa, alive and in front of her, were examples of the good humanity was also capable of doing.

Then it was her turn. Shannon didn't think she would be this emotional, but in the presence of Shiokawa, and Marty, and her family, the tears came at last. She stood next to the flag in its red frame, this piece of her father that was never truly his but someone else's. In truth, it belonged to a family that she hoped still existed, somewhere, in a foreign land she'd never seen. The family of a man her father might have killed, though that answer went to the grave with both of them. As she turned to address Shiokawa, with Tom and Sarah by her side, she knew she was doing the right thing.

"On behalf of my family, we present this flag to you, for you to find its home, where it belongs," Shannon said. "It's been waiting to go home for a long time. This flag reminded my father of a time he didn't want to be reminded of, I think, and I know he's . . . I know he's watching us now and he's happy with what we're doing. He's encouraging us, and he's proud of this."

Shannon paused a moment to collect herself. "I know he would want us to do this," she added, the emotion thick in her voice. "Thank you."

Shiokawa listened closely as Professor Shimojo translated Shannon's words, punctuated by her sniffles. "Thank you very much," Shiokawa answered in kind, and he meant it.

His defensive feelings had melted away, to be replaced by an appreciation he did not anticipate. Shiokawa realized that Marty wanted to return these artifacts with respect to people who'd been on the other side of the war. Though he could not understand Marty's language, Shiokawa understood his feelings. He saw how hard Marty was trying, and the care he had taken to preserve these fragile pieces of history.

Tracing this flag's journey through Japan to the Philippines, to America, and soon back to Japan again, was to observe the life of an object in relation to its surroundings. The flag held two memories, depending on where it was. In America, it trapped the memory of battle and all that encompassed—viewing a person as less than human in order to end a life, hatred for the enemy, following orders, doing whatever was necessary to survive. In Japan, it would embody the person who was lost, the son or brother or nephew or husband; a person with an identity, with a life, with a past but no future. In Japan, it was an extension of family, a spiritual protector, a reminder. In America, it became a reminder of an entirely different kind, of hell rather than home, and depending on the circumstances in which the flag was taken, the worst moments of someone's life and the end of someone else's.

It occurred to Shiokawa that the Japanese soldiers and American soldiers did not fight because they hated each other, but because they had been ordered to do so by their respective countries. That realization was overwhelming, raw, honest. No amount of wartime propaganda on either side could compete with that.

On a Thursday night at the beginning of June, thirty-five days after the meeting in Syracuse, Shannon and Tom received an email.[10] The subject line read, simply, "Kodama's family." The message opened with pleasantries from Shiokawa's office manager, which were followed by seven words that Shannon hadn't been sure she would ever read, punctuated with the same joy she felt.

"We found the family of Mr. Kodama!!!"

CHAPTER 11

FUKUI, JAPAN / 1945

Jinichi Kodama, the middle of three siblings, had a sister and a little brother. Tatsuo, the brother, was an elementary school teacher who had served a short stint as a soldier, from April to August 1937, in the 36th Regiment in the small city of Sabae, located thirty minutes south of their hometown of Fukui. He was called up again on August 11, 1945, to a regiment in the port city of Tsuruga, also in Fukui prefecture, this time an hour south.

Four days later, on August 15, Japan surrendered, ending the war. Tatsuo, discharged on August 31, returned to Fukui to resume life as a teacher.[1]

Yet his hometown was hardly recognizable. On July 19, Fukui had been firebombed by the Americans, their B-29s dropping incendiary devices that destroyed the area and its residents. While taking cover in a bomb shelter during the raid, the three siblings' mother had been killed.[2]

Tatsuo was alive and Jinichi was not. But Tatsuo and his sister had no idea that Jinichi had died until 1948, when the prefecture sent a death notice along with a small wooden box, roughly the width of a modern cell phone, held shut with a metal clasp. The box contained bits of soil and rocks from the Philippines. Until that time, the few surviving relatives had held out hope. Both of Jinichi's parents had died thinking he was alive.

Between Jinichi's actual death and the family's receipt of his death notice, in January 1946, his nephew Takao was born. Tatsuo had married a woman named Tsunako Sasaki and taken the Sasaki family name. And so Takao was born a Sasaki, not a Kodama,

Jinichi Kodama
(courtesy Takao Sasaki)

and he grew up knowing nothing about the story behind his father's original name.

In the years following the war, the family had difficulty finding enough food to survive. Tatsuo and Tsunako, whose family had also suffered loss (both her brothers died in 1938, one of illness, the other in Manchuria), rarely spoke of the war, and Takao did not ask. But that did not stop the war's shadow from looming large over their neighborhood in Fukui. Takao grew up with stories about the firebombing of his hometown. The B-29 bombers had been so close that the faces of the pilots could be seen from the ground. The moat around the prefectural office became so hot that people who jumped in to escape the bombings were boiled to death. The town that had once stood proudly no longer existed.

And every now and then, Takao's mother would talk about the war. Before the American planes came, a large Buddhist temple called Nishibetsuin stood at the center of Fukui. During the air raid, it burned. When that happened, Tsunako told her son, it was like "seeing hell."

While Takao was in elementary school, the Sasaki family continued to struggle to make ends meet. There were no new clothes, only hand-me-downs from relatives. The socioeconomic status of families in Fukui after the war was somewhat diverse, but for the children it did not matter. Takao and his friends played together at school or after school. In his young mind, one distinguishing feature stood out: some of his friends' families served snacks, precious treats such as chocolates or rice crackers. Sometimes Takao would pocket them to take home.

The closest Takao came to interacting with his family history during his schoolboy years involved the Sasaki family gravesite.

Takao was tasked with the upkeep and cleaning of the grave, located in the mountains near Fukui, a job that typically would have gone to his father, Tatsuo. Perhaps because Tatsuo was not a true Sasaki, Takao's maternal grandfather did not trust his son-in-law with the job. Or perhaps the grandchildren, Takao among them, were simply more cherished, and so he was bestowed with the honor.

Starting about ten years after the war, life gradually became easier for the Sasaki family. Takao attended university in Tokyo and got his first job at age twenty-two in 1968. He later returned to the ancestral home in Fukui and worked at a bank. He was back among his family and friends, busy getting married and starting a family of his own.

In 1981, Takao's father, Tatsuo, died at age sixty-four. Takao, thirty-five, had been in denial about his father's poor health. As Tatsuo's health diminished, he began talking more. He wanted to tell his son about the war, about where Tatsuo had been born, about his older brother, Jinichi. Takao wasn't ready to hear it. He was determined that his father would live longer and unwilling to accept that their time together was coming to an end.

When Tatsuo went off to join the forces in Tsuruga in August 1945, he carried a battle flag. Because he never saw combat, the flag came back to Fukui with him, intact. After Tatsuo died, Takao had his father's flag. It was tucked away safely at home, unknowingly awaiting the flag of its original owner's brother, which in 2004 was making its way from America with a man named Shiokawa, thanks to a woman named Shannon.

June 2004

To the Family of Jinichi Kodama:[3]

It is an honor and a privilege to be able to return your Uncle's flag to you. This flag, carried by Jinichi Kodama during World War II, has become such a significant part of our life. After finding the flag, I did months of research about World War II. I discovered the fear, the horror, and the courage in war—and I discovered the "forgotten Heroes." Two of these "forgotten Heroes" I speak of would be your Uncle and my Father—they were young men fighting for their countries and trying to survive savage conditions. Both the Japanese and the Americans sacrificed so much—whether it was losing their life, or surviving, only to come home with the horrific images that would live in their minds and hearts forever. It was because of your Uncle's flag that I realized what my Father had lived with for so many years—and for that I am grateful. Mr. Kodama's flag has become a part of my family history, too.

Your Uncle's flag was cherished after we discovered it. The flag is a constant reminder of two men and two countries who were once enemies—but peace won in the end.

From our family to yours, it is with sincere admiration and respect for your Uncle's bravery and devotion to his country, that we return this piece of your family history to you.

Respectfully Yours,

Thomas and Shannon Moore and the Family of Arthur J. Pim

On July 7, a Wednesday, an email arrived in Shannon's inbox.[4] "Hello from Japan," read the subject line.

To Mr. and Mrs. Thomas Moore

Hello how are you? I hope all of your family are fine.

This is Takao Sasaki, a nephew of Jinichi Kodama. I live in Fukui city which is in the western part of Japan, faced to the Japan sea.

I received the flag from Mr. Shiokawa on June 27. I greatly appreciate your esteemed treat [sic] of the flag.

I can hardly imagine that it has passed 60 years since your father got it.

When I got it in my hand, I was deeply moved. The flag reminded me of my childhood.

My father, who was Jinichi's litter [sic] brother, used to talk to me about him. And moreover the flag gave me precious moment to think about the peace.

We are going to visit his grave on July 17 and tell him about the flag that became a bridge over two countries.

Thank you very much for the kindness.

Respectfully yours,

Takao and Fumiko Sasaki [Fumiko is Takao's wife]

Takao Sasaki (center, striped tie) receives Jinichi Kodama's flag from Masataka Shiokawa (right), June 27, 2004 (courtesy Shannon Moore).

Shannon, still in disbelief over these events, replied four days later. She was full of gratitude that the flag had unlocked a part of her father's life she'd never known, partly revealing an experience that was monumental in shaping the father she loved, yet one he'd never shared with her. She felt closer to him than she ever had, though he'd been gone since 1975. She felt as if the flag was as much a gift to her as it was to Kodama's family.

She would have responded sooner, she told Takao, but had been on vacation with her family. "Your email was the best homecoming surprise I could imagine!" she wrote. "It is truly amazing that after 60 years we have become 'connected' because of a flag."[5] She told the story behind her discovery—of cleaning out her mother's shed the previous summer, and how she thought, because the flag was "so wrinkled and crushed," that it was an old rag. She told him she'd almost thrown it away but stopped at the last second. She wrote about her daughter's Veterans Day school project, and how it had led Shannon to research not only the battle flags but the war in general. She told him how they'd found Professor Shimojo to translate the writing on the flag, and how he'd located Shiokawa's website.

"I would like to express our sincere joy about the flag being back where it belongs," she wrote. "My father never talked about the war. So we really don't know how he acquired it. My mother never knew he had the flag. I believe it was packed away intentionally so my father could forget the horrific images that the war scarred him with. My mother and I truly believe my father would have wanted this flag returned. I believe my father stopped me from throwing the flag into the trash . . . and Uncle Jinichi's flag was meant to be discovered and sent home to you."

Shannon was sure she'd done the right thing. And though she needed no further assurance, she received it from an unexpected source. Her uncle, the one who'd fought at Okinawa, the same one who'd told her, with emotion overflowing and tears running down his face, how horrible it had been, approached her at a family party. He gave her a hug and kiss.

"I think you're doing a wonderful thing," her uncle told her.

To this day, Shannon isn't sure what changed his mind, but she suspects that seeing others who'd been through what he had—Marty and his veteran buddies—making an extraordinary effort to return belongings to the relatives of the deceased showed him that it was okay to let go, to help others, and in doing so, to help free oneself.[6]

Shannon Moore with a photo of her father, 2024 (courtesy Shannon Moore)

July 26th, 2004

Dear Shannon Moore,[7]

I am happy to write to you that the Japanese flag of Mr. Jinichi Kodama was returned to his family (to his nephew) on 27th of June as was promised. We also brought back with us soil and rubble from the land of Leyte, Philippines, to be put in his grave; as we in Japan often say that the dead return to earth, I am sure that Mr. Kodama can now at last lie happily in peace with his parents in the depths of the earth.

May I just say how deeply we appreciate your helping us in our efforts. We could not have come this far had it not been for your cooperation, and my sincere thanks goes also to all the members of your family and to Sarah's friends.

Mr. Kodama was born in Fukui City in Fukui Prefecture in 1914, and his family comprised of his parents, a brother, and a sister, but they had all unfortunately deceased, so the item was returned to his nephew, Mr. Takao Sasaki.

Mr. Kodama apparently worked for a securities company before he joined the army. When the 16th Division was deployed in Leyte Mr. Kodama went there as a lieutenant in charge of many officers. When the Americans landed on Leyte on 20th October 1944, many of the Japanese who were facing a tough fight due to the inefficient supply of goods had already taken refuge in the mountains. From the time the Americans came to Leyte in October until the beginning of December, Mr. Kodama's 16th Division's men had already whittled down to [sic] 18000 to 1500 in number. According to some sources, Mr. Kodama died in the airbase at Brauen on 8th December 1944. This date is the day that the Japanese army made their last counteroffensive against the Americans and many that had made it through until then lost their lives on this day. We can assume that Mr. Kodama shared the same fate as many of his men on this day.

When Mr. Kodama set off for Leyte, he had a wife and an only-child back in his hometown. However, Mr. Kodama was never to return and his only-child seemed to have died soon after the war. His wife, whom we can find no traces off [sic], seems to have left the Kodama family thereafter. The grave of the Kodama family is now being taken care of by Mr. Kodama's younger brother's son, Mr. Takao Sasaki and his daughter Ms. Midori Murota.

Wars, which are started by the egos of those in power, forces [sic] families to part and all that remains from acts of war is grief. Japan has said to have lost three million people in its battles against America. Right now, the politicians in Japan are about to take a path of revising our constitution and follow America into another war. Somehow we must stop this course of action. I too have lost a dear father and have lived these 60 years with the grief that wars bring along with it.

I began this movement because of a tour that a friend took me 28 years ago, in 1977, where he showed me around Okinawa and the air-raid shelter there. Then, even 30 years after the war, there were human bones, articles left by the deceased and unexploded bombs lying on the floor. "How can my father ever rest in peace in this state" were my strong feelings that prompted me to collect items there in Okinawa.

I remember feeling quite shocked to be asked by an American reporter during a press conference in Syracuse about whether I was "proud to have been brought up as a child whose *father died in a war."* Being brought up in a family without a father, with Mum and only myself, it was difficult just to secure the day's food, and even more difficulties had to be overcome to be admitted to schools and even finding employment. My involvement in this movement comes from a deep sense of commitment that I must not let my children and grandchildren go through the same sadness.

For this, we must not let wars be something of the past. I am hoping that by bringing back these artifacts to its [sic] families and by passing down to our people the tragedies of war, it will serve as a roadmap to peace.

My visit to America has connected me to many Americans through the internet, who have expressed that wish to return their artifacts. When I actually see and touch these artifacts, I can feel just how well they were looked after all these 60 years. It touched me deeply to know that one former American soldier had actually looked after very carefully an artifact brought from one's former enemy, and upon expressing his wish to return it to the family of the owner, and actually returning it, he told me that the burden he had carried for 60 years is now off his shoulders. The items were probably taken back to his home country from the battle field as a trophy, but as the years went by, they were kept carefully as a belonging of the war dead. It is perhaps through the item that the notion of enemy and foe became an irrelevant concept for both parties. It made me realize that there too, must have been much suffering and struggles on the side of the American soldiers.

However, when we look at the world around us, we are still witnessing the war in Iraq and others that are bringing *grief to many people. We see almost everyday on our television screens the innocent Iraqi people becoming victims of the war, and American families grieving over their losses of their loved ones in the Iraqi war. The people of America, who are mobilized every time a war is waged, may also be the victims of this act. The world was shocked to see the report of the abuse of Iraqi detainees, which I am sure left people in tense state of shock.*

Needless to say, it is always the weakest in the society who become the greatest victims of war. Those in power will give justification of self-defense to wage a war, but history has proved that almost all these are no more than a war of aggression. These same people in power also know how to evade themselves and their loved ones and relatives to become physically engaged in these wars. We have heard of news that President Bush managed to avoid fighting in the Vietnam War, but during the Second World War, the same kind of thing happened in our country.

I have just given you my honest and straightforward thoughts that I have about wars. I would be interested in finding out how you, Shannon, view this topic from an American point of view.

Perhaps aspiring for a world without war is just too high an ideal, but I am sure that every person who lost their lives in the last war would support this aspiration. It is why I must carry on this journey to not let the war be a thing of the past by returning war items to its owners, and to pledging never to wage another war again to all those who lost their lives in the last one. Through this journey, I hope I would be able to help spread the word of this activity not only in Japan but to America and eventually to the whole world.

Please say hello to your family. Take care and God bless you.

Yours sincerely,
Masataka Shiokawa

FUKUI, JAPAN / MARCH 8, 2023

Takao Sasaki has barely aged. If it weren't for the gray hair where it once shined black, it would be hard to know that nearly twenty years have passed since photographs captured him receiving Jini-chi Kodama's flag in 2004, presented by an equally dark-haired Shiokawa.

Patrick, Kozue, and I have traveled to Fukui by train from Tokyo, one of us more fragile than the others. (Betrayed by a steamed pork bun from an otherwise trusty 7-Eleven, I have been battling food poisoning for two-plus days.) Our hotel on the river allows us a high vantage point to take in this place, as different from the endless sprawl and bustle of Tokyo as just about anywhere I could imagine.

Situated on the opposite side of the island from Tokyo, on Japan's western coast, Fukui City, nestled among forest-covered hills, is the capital of its prefecture. Yet much of the history of its firebombing feels strange to reconcile with the peaceful Fukui of today. The city is covered in, of all things, dinosaurs. One of the main attractions here is a dinosaur museum (which was closed for renovations during our visit, to my husband's dismay)—the largest of its kind in Japan, and among the best in the world, according to several Japanese travel sites. An animatronic trio moves and roars outside the train station, which is also arrayed with images of dinosaurs. One in a white lab coat sits on a bench in the station, inviting photos with seatmates. Where human footprints usually tell travelers where to stand on train platforms, in Fukui it is little dinosaur tracks.

We are taking this in, and I'm trying to convince myself I don't feel nauseous, and then Takao Sasaki is there in the tiny parking lot of the hotel. It is nine in the morning on the dot, our agreed-upon meeting time, a punctuality that would make a shinkansen conductor proud. We manage to Tetris all our luggage and the four of us into his small white Toyota, and he sets out for the Sasaki family home.

Fukui City isn't large, and it doesn't take long before we're in a lovely residential area. From the driver's seat, Takao gestures to a beautiful house on a corner lot. On the front steps, his adult daughter Tomoko greets us; behind Tomoko stands her mother and Takao's wife, Fumiko, her posture hunched slightly with the weight of age. She bows warmly in greeting.

Once inside, we remove our shoes and enter a large, gorgeous traditional room with tatami mats. We lower ourselves to sit on floor cushions, displaying a distressing lack of flexibility that is made all the more prominent by the ease with which Takao and his wife, roughly forty years our senior, comfortably fold their limbs. A low square table is adorned with blue, teal, and white floral teacups on red saucers, and small white plates hold pancakes filled with sweet red bean paste. Fumiko serves steaming green tea, which I sip gratefully. The room is chilled as air seeps in through the edges of the large picture window overlooking the quiet street on what would later become an unseasonably warm day, rising to seventy degrees Fahrenheit. Normally, Takao tells us, there would still be snow.

We talk about our families and our travels and express gratitude for the Sasakis' time and hospitality. To my right, resting atop a shining wooden table, a board is propped against a wall. Fastened to the board with multicolored pushpins is Jinichi Kodama's flag.

When Takao Sasaki smiles, his entire face lights up. He has a wide nose, wispy eyebrows, and plenty of laugh lines around his eyes. His right eye occasionally waters. He gestures animatedly with his hands and is quick to chuckle. Mirth is the word that comes to mind, as though he's a kind spirit.

When the occasion calls for it, he is somber, too. He unfolds a long white sheet of paper: the family tree. He tells us about Jinichi and his grandmother. They were killed within seven months of each other, less than eight months before the war ended.

Nearly eight decades later, the tragic timing of it all would remain with Takao. People's lives can be changed just like that, he thinks, by things completely out of their control. How different it might have been for the Kodama family, and the Sasaki family, and for countless other families, if a few decisions had gone in a different direction—if a city other than Fukui had been bombed that night, if the war had ended sooner, if America had not dropped the atomic bombs. But the war played out as it did, and the bombs fell where they did, in Tokyo and Fukui and Hiroshima and Nagasaki, and the Pacific War ended on August 15, 1945, not before.

The soul stone box that accompanied Jinichi's 1948 death notice sits on the table in front of the flag. It's made from a light-colored and lightweight wood, its construction painfully simple, the metal clasp still intact. Takao had removed the rocks and soil that had been inside and scattered them at Jinichi's grave. Before his death in 1981, Takao's father, Tatsuo—Jinichi's brother—had shown his son the location of the small Kodama family gravesite. No one was left in the Kodama family to look after it.[8]

When Takao was contacted "out of the blue" about the flag, he was shocked.

"Now that this [return] happened, I wish I had heard more of [my father's] stories, but I was busy with my life and never gave it a lot of thought," he says with remorse. "If my father and aunt had lived [twenty] years longer to see the flag returned, they would have gotten together and talked about the old days. At first, I wasn't sure how I felt about getting the flag back, because I didn't know much about it, but when I see Jinichi Kodama's name, I feel that this is my family. I feel that I need to keep it and take care of it."

From beside him, Takao unfolds another flag: that of his father, Tatsuo. Compared to Jinichi's, it appears untouched. The original color is still intact, and it shows very little weathering. There are no stains. This flag did not see battle; it never left the shores of Japan. But the young man who carried it still bore scars, the invisible ones, of loss and hardship and questions unanswered.

The family's butsudan has been concealed behind us this entire time. Takao unfolds himself gracefully from the floor and moves to open it. A smell of incense overpowers the room. The traditional altar is majestic, stunning in detail, the gold immaculately shining. In one of the bottom drawers, Takao typically keeps the flags of the two brothers folded together, at rest—one that never left Japan, the other that took a much longer journey.

There is a photo of Jinichi, too, appearing stoic and handsome in his uniform, which is buttoned to the neck and cinched with a leather belt. Takao takes out another photo, and I smile; I've seen this one. Some seven thousand miles away from Depew, New York, I hold in my hands the picture Masataka Shiokawa took of Shannon and Sarah Moore in 2004, standing next to the flag in its red frame.

Takao isn't sure what he's going to do with Jinichi's grave, he tells us, because he's getting older; in fact, he's not sure what to do

Takao Sasaki and his wife, Fumiko, with the 2004
photograph of Shannon Moore and her daughter Sarah
(photo: Samantha Bresnahan)

with the flags, either. There's a noticeable gap in the connection with the next generation, his daughter, Tomoko, adds. She just doesn't feel it.

"Receiving [these items] could be perplexing, too," Takao says. "It is still fine with my generation, but the next—my daughter's generation—might say, 'What is this?'" He wonders if the local temple will be interested in the flags.

As he speaks, Shannon and Sarah look up at us from the photograph resting on the tabletop. The best hope for Jinichi Kodama, at risk of being lost again, perhaps now lies with a family in America, who will remember his story forever as part of their own.

CHAPTER 12

IWO JIMA / MARCH 12, 2005

Marty Connor stepped onto Iwo Jima for a third time. Sixty years had passed since the first, thirty-five since the second.

After the United States returned Iwo Jima to the Japanese in 1968 as a gesture of goodwill between former enemies that were now allies, there was only one way to visit the island: once a year, Japanese and American veterans and their families could attend a commemorative Reunion of Honor ceremony.[1] With the veterans rapidly aging, it seemed as if the sixtieth anniversary in 2005 would be among the last of the larger milestone gatherings. In two years, Japan would officially rename the island Iō-tō.

Marty traveled with Nick Zingaro, a fellow Iwo Jima veteran and close friend of his from Syracuse.[2] Feeling the urgency of time, Marty had a renewed purpose, and a message. Having reopened a pipeline the previous summer when he met Masataka Shiokawa at the Syracuse airport hotel to hand over twenty items, including the flag from Shannon's father, Marty was more determined than ever to return as many souvenirs as possible to Japan. It felt to him like unfinished business.[3]

As they had in 1970 and at subsequent reunions on Iwo Jima, many of the veterans retraced their steps, revisited pivotal locations from their time on the island, relived visceral memories. For some it was cathartic; for others it was a struggle; for many it was both.

Teddy Draper was among the first-timers to revisit the island.[4] A Navajo code talker, Draper had been assigned to the Fifth Marine Division. He landed on Iwo on February 19 and the next day was nearly killed on the beach by a mortar, which temporarily blinded and deafened him.[5] But with few Navajo still alive to send radio messages, Draper was rushed to the medics, got fixed up, and went back to work. Three days later, he would be the one who sent out the message as the Americans raised the flag on Mount Suribachi.[6] In 2005, he brought his own American flag, raised it up a pole with the help of a Marine, and saluted it.

Others wandered through the elaborate network of tunnels burrowed into the terrain, a string of dangling lights illuminating the way. Rusted bits of canisters remained preserved in the earth, reminders of what had happened there sixty years before. The integrity of the layered bunkers, pillboxes, and tunnels, which covered roughly eleven linear miles of an island that measured only eight square miles, was beginning to fail.[7] It was another reminder of the passing of time; soon, many of the tunnels and bunkers would become too unsafe to visit, so Japan closed them, meaning anything or anyone that remained would be forever interred.

On Iwo that day was an attendee who, though small in stature, was as notable as any of the dignitaries from either the Japanese or American delegation. Just shy of her seventy-fourth birthday, she was fondly known as Rosa. But she had been born as Chikako—Tsunezo Wachi's daughter.[8]

The young girl who had listened to the emperor's stunning declaration of defeat on a crackling radio after fleeing Tokyo in 1945, who had been delighted to learn that her father had survived the war yet shocked to welcome home not a naval captain but a Buddhist reverend, had picked up where her father left off after his death in early 1990. Letters addressed to Reverend Wachi or Captain Wachi continued to arrive long after he died, and Rosa Ogawa was sometimes the one who responded to them. She struck up correspondences across the Pacific using the English she had learned as a girl and perfected as an adult, having taught the language to young students in Japan for decades, just like her mother.

Other influences from her parents featured prominently in Rosa's life: having strengthened her Christian faith over the years, Rosa remained a devout Catholic. She was a wife, a mother, and, by 2005, a grandmother. She had a self-described "addiction" to knitting. When someone died, she had a fondness for the phrase "changed his habitat from here to eternity." And she had helped facilitate the return of artifacts from former enemies.

Six months before the reunion, in September 2004, Rosa typed an email after watching a special on the Japanese public media broadcaster NHK. "I was glad to see you very well working in vim and vigor with other cooperators for the bereaved families of Japanese war victims," she wrote to the recipient. "I believe, as you say, my late Dad would be satisfied and grateful that his wish has been pursued by the ex-combatants of both nations with Iwo Jima as their common denominator."

In keeping with her custom of commenting on the weather with an elegance befitting a lifelong student of English, she added, "I hope you'll enjoy your beautiful autumn in your area. When I think of autumn in the northeastern part of the US, I imagine that of the scene described in the poems of my favorite Robert Frost. Is your autumn as beautiful as that?" She closed by thanking the recipient for his efforts in pursuit of "your humanitarian activity."

The email was addressed to Marty Connor.

After Tsunezo Wachi had died, one of the letters Rosa responded to in his stead was from Marty. During the holiday season of 1999, nearly a decade after her father had passed away, Rosa sent a Christmas card from Tokyo addressed to the house on the hill in Syracuse, New York, the front adorned with two white cranes in flight against a blue and golden backdrop—a reproduction of a painting by Japanese artist Eizo Kato.

"How's everything been with you?" Rosa asked on the back flap of the card, the inside reserved for season's greetings and her customary sign-off, "Love and prayers." She shared her regrets that photos Marty had sent to her father on behalf of another American veteran had not yet been successfully identified and returned to surviving relatives. "I hope, however, they'll be claimed by the bereaved families," she continued, in the "near future."

So began the communication between two members of different generations affected by the war: a combatant and a descendant of one. (In reality, Marty and Rosa were far closer in age—separated by just five years—than Marty and his wartime counterpart, Wachi.[9]) Finding common ground in their shared Catholic faith, Rosa and Marty exchanged well-wishes around the Christmas and Easter holidays and updates on family; occasionally Marty requested help with a return.

He was far from Rosa's only pen pal.[10] She was a prolific correspondent, adept at keeping up the cross-Pacific relationships her father had started, mostly with US Marines, and also building connections of her own. She attended reunions on Iwo Jima when she could. Her English-language skills allowed her, like her father, to chat directly with American veterans, their families, history buffs, and other visitors to a greater extent than some of the other Japanese attendees were able to. All the while, she was motivated by the mission of her father, determined to carry on his legacy, and in doing so, she forged one of her own, characterized by kindness and compassion.

In December 2004, just months before the sixtieth reunion at Iwo Jima, Rosa sent Marty another Christmas message, this one on a card bearing a springtime image of Mount Fuji surrounded by cherry blossoms. "I'm looking forward to the visit to Iwo Jima next March," she wrote, "to trace the tracks of those who sacrificed their precious lives for the cause of the nations and pursue Dad's will to keep friendships between our nations."

During the 2005 reunion, atop Suribachi, against a clear blue sky, Marty came across Kiyoshi Endo, a former Japanese naval lieutenant and one of the few Japanese veterans to attend that year. Endo was the chairman of the Japanese Iwo Jima Veterans Association.

Bowing his head slightly, Marty introduced himself, adding, "I'm the one that's sending you the flags."

Marty Connor on Iwo Jima for a third time, attending the Reunion of Honor in March 2005 (courtesy Connor family)

His hand still clasping Marty's, Endo turned to an interpreter standing by his side and listened.

"He's receiving a lot of mail," the interpreter relayed to Marty.

"Alright," Marty said, still shaking hands. "We gave you five flags today and a picture. We'll send more."

Endo thanked him with a bow.[11]

A nearby reporter asked Endo how he felt. As Marty looked on, Endo spoke through his interpreter: "To be together like this where we fought sixty years ago, when we hated each other—now all our hate is gone. To be together like this, it's an honor."

"Tell him," Marty implored, "I feel the same way. We feel the same way."

Though it was not on display on Iwo's sacred sands, Marty Connor had an ego. He always had, and his children will be the first to tell you this.[12] His wife, Janet, would concur, eyes twinkling. Competitions were drummed up at every opportunity, within the family and even with the neighbors. Marty, Janet, and their friends up the street played an annual tennis tournament they dubbed the "Memorial Day Classic." Marty also competed with the same friend, who hailed from Sicily, over who had the better tan.

Janet was up for anything Marty threw at her—buying a stake in Labrador Mountain, where they loved to ski, and putting it in Janet's name; attending endless Marine Corps reunions and functions, both in the United States and abroad; finding a place in their house for a steady stream of battlefield mementos.

Yet about his mission to return war artifacts, Marty remained humble. He did not boast about it, though he did spread the word, but only in service of finding more items to return. Perhaps the undertaking contained an element of competition with himself. And in this effort, Janet was a key part of his support system. She had gone back to school for her insurance license to help out at the firm, and without missing a step, she once again met him stride for stride in this project. They had their own language, and it extended to the return efforts. Marty, in his later years, unwilling to get comfortable using a computer, leaned on Janet once more. She printed every email Marty received, and he wrote out his response on paper in pencil, which Janet dutifully typed and sent.

This went on for years, because Marty's endeavors were beginning to pay off. At all the reunions he dragged his family to, he met more veterans. Articles by Sean Kirst that appeared from time to time in the Syracuse *Post-Standard* were picked up by national newspaper wires. In these ways, word about his return project spread. For some veterans who heard about Marty's mission, it was the opportunity for reconciliation they had been searching for all those years.

For all the veterans who did not agree with Marty's efforts, who refused to purchase a Japanese-made car or eat at a sushi restaurant, who sneered words like "Jap," there were many who were drawn to his mission. One of those men was Bob Cudworth.

Four years older than Marty, Bob was born on August 7, 1922, near Cortland, New York, south of Syracuse.[13] While attending Syracuse University, Bob enlisted in the Marine Corps in 1943. He was selected for Officer Candidate School in Quantico, Virginia, and eventually assigned to the 3rd Marine Division. Captain Cudworth served on Guam, helping to secure the island before being shipped out to Iwo Jima, where he landed on the fifth day of the battle.[14]

Bob said he never took any souvenirs of his own, but he watched it happen all around him. The Japanese flags and swords were most popular. Ordered back to Guam after surviving Iwo Jima, Bob and a few other Marines were climbing up the cargo nets to board their ship. One of the men was carrying a Japanese flag, complete with red circle and black personalized ink markings, which he'd had for probably two or three weeks. As he scaled the cargo nets, he dropped it, and it fluttered down into the sea. He looked at it longingly, and Bob saw the stark disappointment all over his face. "Forget it," Bob told the young man. "We're not stopping to get that flag out of that water."

Decades later, Bob met Marty at an Iwo Jima anniversary event in Syracuse. The two men realized they had a lot in common, and they struck up a friendship. Marty told Bob about his postwar mission, explaining that he had been asking fellow veterans and their family members to return souvenirs taken from Pacific battlefields. He said these items held a special meaning for surviving relatives in Japan, and that returning them could provide something akin to closure, even after all this time. It was a noble cause, Bob thought, and while he personally did not have any items to send back, he wanted to help. Marty had just the task for him.

Bob had been a newspaper writer and editor. He had a natural way with words that Marty felt he himself did not possess.[15] So Marty enlisted Bob's help, and together they sent articles to Marine Corps publications, including *Leatherneck Magazine*, and to magazines and newsletters of the 3rd, 4th, and 5th Marine Divisions, urging people to return their spoils of war.

The publicity added to the occasional coverage from local media, resulting in a profile in the *New York Times* and eventually a documentary that aired around the world on CNN International.[16] Though interviews made Marty nervous, he wanted to spread the word any way he could.

Marty had a deep respect for reporter Sean Kirst of the *Post-Standard*, and it went both ways. Sean was a fellow Central New Yorker, born in Dunkirk, which he described as a little factory town outside Buffalo—not far from where Shannon Moore lived. He started working at the *Post-Standard* in 1988. A cousin of Marty's also worked at the paper. One day, the cousin casually mentioned Marty's endeavors to return war souvenirs to Japan, without realizing Sean's connection to the war: he was the son of a Pacific veteran, a man whom Sean described as "emotionally wounded" by the experience.

IWO JIMA VETERANS ! !

Many of us still have in our possession LISTEN UP! **pictures, letters & other personal items we took as souvenirs some 54 years ago and today they have little importance to us.**

These same items would mean everything to the wives, children and grandchildren of the Japanese who did not return.

If you have artifacts you would be willing to return, the person to send them to is:

KIYOSHI ENDO   or   **MARTIN C. CONNOR***

One of the ads placed by Marty Connor to fellow Iwo Jima veterans (courtesy Connor family)

Sean was immediately enthralled by the idea of Marty and his mission, of this "gray-haired vet sending stuff back to Japan." Their introduction inspired what would become several columns written by Sean about Marty and his other Syracuse veteran buddies banding together with unlikely allies across the ocean. Sean was present at the meeting between Shannon Moore and Masataka Shiokawa at the Syracuse airport hotel in 2004. He felt the weight of the translated words of the poem from Okinawa: "In the blood, flowers bloom"—from something horrible, something beautiful.

What stuck with Sean over the years as he covered the story was Marty's businesslike demeanor, which Sean considered "a veneer over a very big heart."[17] As no-nonsense as Marty was about his return mission, as much as he insisted to Sean and other journalists that it was simply the right thing to do, Sean sensed in Marty a deep "reservoir of soul."

That's why the story never got old, he said. It only ever got better.

The letters began to arrive, some typed, some handwritten. Then the emails.[18] Many started the same way: *Dear Mr. Connor.*

"I saw the article about you in the Post-Standard," one began, dated November 15, 2010, "and as a matter of conscience, I am enclosing two personal pictures that I acquired on the island of Ie Shima in April of 1945. They have writing on the back, and one is especially sad because it is of a family."

Handwritten in blue pen on lined, three-hole-punched notebook paper, dated February 10, 2000: "I am sending the dog tag I found on Iwo Jima."

Typed, sent from Liverpool, New York, and dated December 8, 1999: "I'm enclosing a couple of items that I believe I acquired from Iwo Jima, but since I was at the invasion of Saipan also they could have come from there. Its been so long since I've looked at them I cannot remember where I picked them up. You are offering a worthy service and I hope you have much success."

Dated November 15, 2010: "I read the article about Japanese memorabilia in the Post Standard. I never served in the service but I found this Japanese flag in the attic when I moved in."

An email, sent from Missouri on May 16, 2011: "I applaud your efforts to get personal effects back to the families of WWII soldiers. My father served in WWII and brought back several souvenirs that I have often wondered what to do with."

The previous day, another email, this time from California: "I have longed to return a Japanese battle flag to the soil of Japan.

This flag was in our family from a relative's belongings who also died during the war. My hope is the flag makes its way back to the Japanese soldier's family where it belongs."

May 14, 2011, from Bozeman, Montana: "I just read your article on cnn.com. I have my uncle's souvenir from Iwo Jima. Inside is a letter, a hand fan, a cigarette, a couple fishing hooks, and a pouch of some sort."

The same day, an email from Kennebunkport, Maine: "My dad was in the 4th Marine Division and landed on Iwo Jima on his 21st birthday. . . . He too had a number of souvenirs from the battle, but I never knew about them until I found them after he passed away. . . . Among the items are a number of letters that may be of importance to some family members—they are still in envelopes that are addressed. . . . I would be so happy if a family could read the words of their loved one. I've hung on to them all this time hoping that some day I could find a way to send them to the appropriate party."

From Wisconsin, June 28, 2011: "I have a Japanese battle flag that my father brought home from the South Pacific at the end of WWII. He was a marine who served in many of the battles (though not Iwo Jima). It most likely came from Guadalcanal. My father passed away last summer and this is one of those items we didn't know how to handle. After reading the article, we do."

May 13, 2011: "About a year ago a friend of mine gave me some Japanese artifacts that his father had collected while he was in the Marines fighting in the Pacific. . . . I am a former Marine and veteran of the Persian Gulf War which is why my friend gave me the artifacts. Being a Marine and combat veteran

I know that I would like for my family to have my personal effects returned."

An email from a judge in Iowa, May 13, 2011: "My father passed away four years ago, but I know he would have liked those items returned to the soldier's family if possible."

September 28, 2013, from the daughter of a veteran from Utah: "We have been going through my father's things, and found the flag he seemed to be ashamed of having. He only had it out once that I remember, and said he wasn't proud of it. He was stationed in the Philippines for a while. . . . Are you still taking items for repatriation? . . . Thank you for your time, and especially for your mission."

November 5, 2012: "I apologize that it has taken me a month to get the flag in the mail, but I wanted to talk with my grandfather about my intentions to ensure that he was absolutely okay with me sending the flag to you. He is. . . . The flag is remarkable. It may even have some decades-old blood on it, but you know and have taught others that its true value lies in the family or other important history described by the characters inscribed on the flag."

June 21, 2011, with the subject line "War Trophies": "Your humanity has deeply touched me and altered my thinking. My father fought in the Chinese theater, serving in the 14th Army Air Force, and I think if he were alive today, he would also be happy to know that finally, peace prevails among yesterday's enemies."

In a time before social media, the grassroots nature of Marty's efforts resonated with the veteran community. It did not hurt that the call to action was coming from a fellow Marine, himself a veteran of not just any battle, but of Iwo Jima. Among the worst of the worst. That meant something.

One of the letters Marty received was from a man named Keith Bernard, who lived in Louisiana. Keith's father, Joe Bernard, was born in 1923 and, upon graduating from Peters High School, joined the Marines after Pearl Harbor. Young Joe was dispatched to some of the most brutal battles the Pacific Theater had to offer: Guadalcanal, Saipan, Tinian, Iwo Jima.[19] In the middle of the fighting, after two-plus months on Guadalcanal and beyond, Joe was sent home to a naval hospital in New Orleans to recover from malaria. His hero's homecoming was fodder for the local newspaper, but not just because the private had temporarily returned from war.[20]

Under a headline that read, "Jap Yells at Joe, but Joe, a [New Orleans] Boy, Shoots First; Jap Swallows Yell," the story began with this scene: "'I cut your guts out,' the fierce-looking Jap lieutenant yelled at Pvt. Joe Bernard, rushing at him with a sword. Joe yelled back, but he fired as he yelled. He has the sword as a souvenir."

The quiet twenty-one-year-old had "personally accounted" for seven Japanese soldiers, including the lieutenant who had charged him. The man was Koichi Fujihara, the newspaper said, his name known from the photo Joe had taken off his dead body, along with the sword "and other souvenirs."

Joe's souvenirs were so impressive that the collection was on display at the Roosevelt Hotel in New Orleans, guarded "day and night" by two Marines. Items included a signed battle flag, paper money, coins, a "sacred amulet," a Japanese stamp, and pictures of Japanese soldiers "taken off their dead bodies." A photo of the display topped the newspaper story. The caption, written at the height of wartime, held nothing back: "These Japanese souvenirs, most of them taken off the bodies of Japs personally liquidated by Pfc. Joseph Bernard, United States Marines."

"He didn't like talking about his exploits," the reporter continued, "but the information was dragged out of him little by little."

That quietness was a trait Keith remembers about his father, who was reluctant to talk much about his experience during the war, even long after it had ended. But when he did share war stories, often around Keith's uncles, who were fellow veterans of the Second World War, they stuck with Keith. Many of the stories were graphic, not meant for small eavesdropping ears—for example, stories of "banzai" charges. Keith learned that Joe got malaria because of the swarms of buzzing insects everywhere; they were drawn to "stacks of dead bodies in the sun." It was so bad that before Joe could eat his food, his young son overheard, he had to blow flies off his spoon.

The aftermath of the war went beyond stories. When Joe married Keith's mother in 1948, he was committed to go on a nightly patrol of his own making, walking the perimeter of the neighborhood looking for "odd cars" before he was able to settle in to sleep.

Among the items Joe had taken were two postcards from dead soldiers on Guadalcanal, the Japanese writing faded with time. Both were addressed to a Mr. Shuichirou Kikuchi, but they were from two different senders. They contained prayers for good health and updates on "a great deal of tension," even in the countryside, away from Tokyo.[21]

PFC Joe Bernard, "home on leave with malaria," 1943 (courtesy Keith Bernard)

Keith was not quite ready to part with the flag his father had brought home and posed with so proudly in front of the fireplace, prized sword also on display. Keith associated the flag with his father; its image was conjured in his mind's eye when he thought of Joe. But the postcards—the idea of returning them or sending them to where they'd never arrived appealed to Keith. He wasn't quite sure how his father would feel about it, a man who "hated the [Japanese] fighting men . . . no doubt about it," according to his son. But maybe, Keith thought, he would have softened his stance over time.

Either way, though Keith would have given anything to sit down with his father as an adult and hear all his stories, Joe was no longer here to offer an opinion. And so, ten days after Veterans

Day, on November 21, 2014, Keith wrote a letter to Marty Connor on a piece of trifold graph paper.

> *Mr. Connor—*
>
> *Enclosed are two postcards my father Joseph A. Bernard, 2nd Division, USMC, picked up on Guadalcanal 1942.*
>
> *I cannot find the photographs he had, hopefully I can find them and send them to you.*
>
> *The local story in our hometown newspaper named the Japanese Lt. Koichi Fujihara. He led a 10-man squad who were all killed by the Marines.*
>
> *I hope that you can locate family in Japan through your contact.*
>
> *Interesting enough, my dad brought back Lt. Fujihara's sword but gave it to a neighborhood kid when he got back from the Pacific.*
>
> *I enjoyed writing to you and meeting you through this correspondence.*
>
> *Thanks—Keith Bernard*

He tucked the postcards inside the graph paper, affixed a stamp with an American flag to a plain white envelope, and mailed it north from New Orleans to Syracuse. It was a start, Keith thought. If that was successful, perhaps the flag too. But not just yet.

CHAPTER 13

On a clear, crisp Thursday, Masataka Shiokawa had a different postcard in hand as he strode purposefully toward an office building in Maebashi, a city in Gunma prefecture, central Japan. While others were bundled in layers to ward off the chill, Shiokawa was dressed in only a suit, shirt, and tie. He had no time for the cold; he'd been waiting for this day for some eight years.

Yellowed with age but otherwise well preserved and covered in vibrant ink strokes, the postcard in his possession had been written in the early 1940s by a man named Rihachiro Shizuka to his wife, Hatsue, with whom he shared a son. From his barracks in Heilongjiang, northern China, he had described the heat, but added, "It's nothing compared with the heat my fellow soldiers [are] fighting under in southern Pacific islands."[1]

Rihachiro was shipped to the Marshall Islands before he was able to send the postcard, so he kept it with him, waiting for the next opportunity. But his chance would never come; he was killed in 1944, his postcard pocketed by someone else, not unlike the postcards taken by US Marine Joe Bernard, from New Orleans.[2]

More than fifty years later, Rihachiro's postcard would resurface in a warehouse with other artifacts, discovered by Shiokawa. It would take another eight years before Shiokawa could track down a surviving family member, with the help of a local government officer, after almost giving up when the national authorities told him they could not find anyone, despite the address written on the postcard. Shiokawa's perseverance paid off, and now that meeting was finally taking place.

Rihachiro's younger brother, Torao Shizuka, age eighty-five, had a round face and white hair. He'd agreed to meet Shiokawa in Maebashi to receive the postcard in person. Seated next to his son, Toshio, Torao reached out as Shiokawa gently slid the card to him across a plain, wooden conference-room table. The youngest of the three boys, Torao had lost both his older brothers in the war, and he had nothing of Rihachiro's in his possession. He fondly remembered Rihachiro as energetic and active. Surprised not only that the postcard existed, but that Shiokawa had it and was able to return it to him, Torao vowed to "keep it in good care."

The Shizuka family were farmers, he told Shiokawa. The brothers' education had focused on "the way the military worked and thought," as was the case for all schoolchildren growing up in imperial Japan.

"The war was a fight between countries," Torao said, "so we the ordinary people did not know exactly what was going on. In my time, it was so natural that all boys joined the military when they became of age. It was a secondary question if you might die once you joined the military. You would say today it's so ridiculous that you were forced to go to the war and die. But the education we were given then was to work and fight for the country."

For young boys like him and his brothers, he added, the war was "nothing we could resist."

Torao had watched his older brothers ship out—the entire town showing up to wish them well, as it did for every departing soldier and sailor, waving flags and cheering until the train was no longer in sight. When Torao's time came, he ended up in the Imperial Navy, fortunate enough never to be sent beyond Japan's shores.

"When the war finished," he remembered, "I thought, 'Oh, I do not have to go to the place where bullets were shot.' I was relieved." He had been just nineteen or twenty years old; of his exact age, he couldn't be sure, but the feeling of profound relief resurfaced as clearly as it had sixty-six years ago.

All those years later, after bidding goodbye to Torao and his son, a piece of their lost family history returned at last, Shiokawa was the one who was relieved. A "heavy responsibility" lifted from his shoulders, he felt light and energized by seeing Torao's happiness at receiving such an unexpected gift. It built momentum to keep him fighting for the next case, and the one after that, and on and on, whether it took eight days or eight years to find the rightful owner of each artifact.

As always, Shiokawa's own father was never far from his mind. Rihachiro's postcard mentioned his young son, just as the postcards that came for nearly a year to Shiokawa's mother from his father had done, making the letters the piece of his father Shiokawa had clung to all those years. He knew exactly what that felt like, what it meant. And he felt grateful for his own sons, who often looked after his insurance business, affording him the chance to focus on what he considered to be his most important work.

"Many of our fathers died while thinking about their families," Shiokawa reflected after the meeting with Torao on that chilly February day. "They cannot say anything anymore. If I can do a little to help deliver the voice of those who lost their lives in pain . . . ," he trailed off. "I delivered one today."

For the longest time, Shiokawa had been on his own in his recovery efforts. What had begun with his first trip to Okinawa in 1977 would repeat many times as he made solo trips to the island for the purposes of recovering human remains and, later, artifacts as well. Married with four sons, he occasionally took some of his children along on his trips, which would eventually number over 150. But he wanted to reach even more people and expand the impact of his recovery efforts.

That's where the NPO came in. His association included the children and grandchildren of Japan's war dead, as well as veterans of the war and civilians who had lived through it. A group member suggested that the younger generations needed not only to know what had happened, but to witness firsthand the physical and emotional scars left by war. And so began the next phase of Shiokawa's quest.

On February 11, 2005, nearly a year after Shiokawa met Marty and Shannon in Syracuse, a group of thirty-three Japanese from all over the country, ranging in age from twenty to eighty, joined him in Naha, Okinawa, for a two-day tour of the battlefields.[3] They visited a bunker, where a veteran of the battle addressed them, a sobering experience that shifted the demeanor of all the tour participants. They dug for remains using shovels and rakes but came up empty-handed.

Still, Shiokawa measured success in another crucial way. Tour participants were overwhelmed by their experiences: "To think that they hid and lived in a place like this." "I saw the reality of war." "By coming here, I realized that our comfortable and peaceful lives are founded on the ultimate sacrifices of the war dead." "I want to pass on this experience." "By never repeating the tragedy of war, we respectfully commemorate (the war dead)." Shiokawa, who had been living with similar sentiments his entire life, found their responses a validation of his work, and they fueled the fire of his obsession. As the tour group excavated the earth, a hope always remained in his heart: at any moment, perhaps just a shovelful of dirt away, maybe they would find his own father.

A year later, almost to the day, he returned to Okinawa with another group. They searched through a trench bunker in the former Ōzato village, today known as Nanjo, located in south-central Okinawa. This time, the group was more successful, finding four sets of skeletal remains, an identification tag from the Imperial Army's 4152nd Unit, a personal seal with a name, and more artifacts.

It was a profound movement of ordinary citizens stepping up to fill a need many of them felt had not been handled properly through more official channels. Nor was the movement reliant on citizens of a foreign land—on the return of stolen objects from America. It was organic, as if the very earth called to them, telling them what—and who—it held.

After a story on their efforts ran in the local news, a survivor of the 4152nd came forward. The bunker, he said, had been destroyed by the Americans on May 24, 1945. He had lived to tell the tale by pure luck, having been positioned against a wall in the bunker.

Several of the artifacts found by the group were identified and returned to the families. The success of the mission caused forty-five participants to sign up for the tour the following year, in 2007. From January 19 to 21, the tour group examined the bunker in Ōzato again. There were special guests in their midst: family members of the soldier whose identification tag had been found there the year before. Knowing how it felt to receive that gift, perhaps they could help others feel the same. In the bunker, a Buddhist priest read the sutras.

The tours continued year after year. On tour four, which had forty participants in two locations, they found nine partial or nearly whole skeletal remains, a gun holster, ammunition, and other artifacts. On tour five, in November 2008, thirty-three people found twenty-seven remains, as well as wristwatches, pocket watches, hand grenades, and shoes.

Tours six, seven, eight, and nine yielded even more skeletal remains and personal objects, resulting in more returns to more families—and more participants having firsthand experiences in the field. The seventh tour, in 2011, was the first to have zero participants who had lived through the war themselves. "We felt the weight of the 66 years that had passed since the end of the war," Shiokawa wrote. That was made even more true when the group uncovered fifty sets of remains in a bunker surrounded by thickets, located in Kohatsu, near the island's eastern coast.

The eighth tour included someone who matched Shiokawa's passion for the cause, a man who'd been born in Okinawa and raised among its dead. His name was Takamatsu Gushiken.

A dental equipment repairman by day and a human remains recovery specialist at night and on weekends, Gushiken lived and breathed the terrain of Okinawa, having grown up among its graveyard. Trained to handle unexploded bombs and grenades, he was trying to right unresolved wrongs. Both attributes are handy. In the caves of Okinawa, you never know what you might find.

Okinawa is not large. In essence, it is one mass grave. The immense scale of the violence earned the battle a moniker: "tetsu no ame"—typhoon of steel.[4] Decades later, lush vegetation has reclaimed the land, the terrain again covered in green, years' worth of fallen waxy, emerald leaves in the hills turning brown and returning to the earth as soil. The overgrowth hides the violent past of a land that was once cleaved open by the rain of metal falling from the sky. Okinawan and American and Japanese bones rest there, some in seated positions, as Gushiken has observed, frozen where they fell, a macabre time capsule that cannot be unseen and should not be ignored.

During the rainy season in the subtropical climate on the island, torrential downpours can drown out any attempt at normal conversation. Rain splatters loudly on the jungle leaves. The faint paths up into the hills turn so slippery that it's easy to imagine how one misstep might contribute to the island's bone count. Gushiken was often on the hunt for bones—bone fragments, whole skeletons, and partial skeletons. It was a mission of sorts that grew from humble beginnings into what could only be described as a battle of wills with the Japanese government itself. For years, the official party line had been that the human remains recovery effort on the island of Okinawa was complete. Tell that to Gushiken, who spent countless hours combing the caves littering the jungle terrain. Tell that to the skeleton he shined his flashlight on in a crevice in the hillside.

Takamatsu Gushiken was born in Naha, Okinawa's capital city, in 1954, less than a decade after the bloodiest battle of the Pacific War ended on the same soil. Hundreds of thousands died, many of them innocent Okinawans drafted into war by the Japanese. Gushiken grew up in the island's hills, playing in the grasses with his friends as a boy. He remembered tripping on bones overgrown by a bush and seeing a skull still covered by a helmet. He was scared—and curious. But he was told not to touch it, because one day the dead soldier's family might come searching for the body.

That idea stuck with Gushiken. When he was twenty-eight years old, a friend who was a member of a group that occasionally searched for remains on Okinawa asked him if he'd like to participate. Gushiken had already been thinking about how he could help those who'd been lost, like the skeleton in the helmet he'd seen as a child. His first search with the group yielded several remains, bones retrieved from the earth. But it was haunting.

In the car on the way home from the field that day, Gushiken thought he'd never be able to search again. Yet when the group asked him to join them the next year, he remembered that most of the people in the search party had been elderly, often the mother or father of the deceased.

"Remembering those old people going up the hills with a waddling gait wearing a rain jacket, rake in hand, I thought, I was younger than them," Gushiken reflected.[5]

Despite his uneasiness and the memories of all those bones from the previous year, he agreed to go. It was the beginning of what would become his life's work, the path that would eventually lead him to Shiokawa.

In Okinawa, it is nearly impossible to escape the battle, even six-plus decades later. Evidence of it is quite literally buried in plain sight. Construction and urban development bring the issue to the surface with each new dig. In 2007, one legendary battle site was flattened for, of all things, military housing.[6] Upon visiting the site, Gushiken could "see some of the bones from the soil." Horrified, he called a local government office. Instead of agreeing

Takamatsu Gushiken, Okinawa, April 2018
(photo: Samantha Bresnahan)

to recover the remains before allowing construction to continue, officials had a barrier erected around the site. Later, some of the truck drivers who worked on the project told Gushiken they could see bones among the soil headed for a landfill.

Okinawa's ghosts continued crying out from the ground. In early 2021, excavation at a site designated for a new national park uncovered more bones, believed to be remains from the battle. Gushiken had found remains in the same location a few months earlier. Meanwhile, the Okinawa Defense Bureau was "procuring dirt" on the southern part of the island, near Itoman, for construction of a new base. Gushiken, concerned that more remains lay scattered in the earth there, pressed the bureau to call off its plans.[7]

If no one else would search for the remains, then he would, Gushiken figured. He trekked into the hills in the rain. He rigged up a bucket on a pulley system to ferry bones from deep in the earth. He was not there to collect bones and artifacts as souvenirs, as some people did—digging up old guns and grenades and even vials of morphine, the liquid preserved inside. In the larger caves, part of the underground network the Japanese built to fortify the island before the battle, items were still left behind, signs of lives once lived. Protecting the caves from souvenir hunters was another element of Gushiken's work.

It was a lonely effort. It took time away from his own family. By the late 2010s, he was in his mid-sixties. He was tired. But Gushiken was too far in to stop now. He founded a nonprofit agency and had some volunteer help from time to time, but it remained mostly a one-man operation.

Gushiken was small in stature, which was helpful for this line of work. Time and time again, he slipped easily into tiny caves, which were often only large enough for one man. The light from his headlamp illuminated the caves' interiors. It was eerily silent, the rain, so prominent just inches away, completely muffled. In one cave, to which I accompanied him, human remains were clearly visible. Someone had died there. His body was still there. Gushiken picked up two small, thin bones in his right hand and held them against his outstretched left arm. He put them down gently and tapped the inside of his forearm, saying without words that this was part of the man's—or boy's—skeleton.

Gushiken carried a tattered red anatomy book in his knapsack. It helped him identify the bones, though he rarely needed to consult it anymore. He also had a book of sketches showing Japanese soldiers' clothing and gear. In that cave, he found small metal discs with holes in their centers—from the soldier's poncho. There was the rusted bottom of what was likely a can of food. And there was an unexploded grenade.

Japanese grenades were square-shaped compared with their round American counterparts. Their exterior resembled a metal pineapple skin. Gushiken theorized that this soldier had not died by suicide, as the grenade was still intact and Gushiken did not see a sword. Most of the metal items in the cave had withstood the passing of time, protected from the natural elements. Most likely the soldier died from injuries sustained in an attack.

Other than that, who was he? A man? Or a boy? Mainland Japanese? Or Okinawan? Did he have a wife, or children?

There were clues. To Gushiken, those were the most important discoveries of all. At the end of the day, his mission was about identity and dignity and family. Who was missing this man? Where was his home? And could Gushiken help him get back there, to find his final resting place, to finally be at peace?

It's what I would want if that were me, Gushiken thought. It was how he'd want someone to treat his body, and his family, had he been born just two decades earlier and been conscripted into the Japanese military ahead of the American invasion and died here on this small Pacific island.

The best clues were the most obvious ones—forms of identification like dog tags, which listed the soldier's name. In those cases, Gushiken consulted the registry and searched for a region with the family name.

By 2018, he had made four successful identifications—one thanks to an engraved fountain pen he'd found with a body in a bunker near Naha in 2010—out of recovered remains averaging roughly a hundred bodies a year. Sometimes he could narrow the identity down to a few possibilities. Once, two families showed up for a memorial service, just in case. Sometimes the families were not interested at all. When he wasn't 100 percent sure he had found the right family, he told them that up front. More often than not, they came anyway.

The vast majority of remains could not be identified. Gushiken initially took the bones to a morgue for safekeeping, only to learn that they weren't safe there. The morgue soon ran out of room and began cremating remains Gushiken was actively working to identify. He pointed out to officials at the morgue, none too gently, that they were cremating remains without the families' consent. His protests stopped the practice, and the remains were instead "temporarily enshrined." Still, he feared the cremations would resume.

By then, at least, he'd found Masataka Shiokawa, a kindred spirit. Having met during Shiokawa's 2012 tour of Okinawa to search for remains, the two men had formed a bond.

Like Shiokawa, the Okinawan preaches a message of peace, of never again, of the power of remembrance. In some ways, the remembering is more prominent in Okinawa, where remains can be unearthed at any time, by anyone, at any age. "When you have seen the bones," Gushiken told a group of elementary students in 2009, "you can say that [Okinawa] was a battle site. . . . Think, when you grow up, could such a terrible thing happen again?"[8]

What had started for Shiokawa as a lonely endeavor eventually expanded into a village of support that extended from Saga to Tokyo to Okinawa, across the sea to the United States, and even elsewhere in Asia. No matter where Shiokawa went or whom he spoke to, whether veterans or survivors, the sentiment was often the same: a profound disbelief that Japan had ever entered into war against the United States to begin with.

Besides making annual trips to Okinawa, Shiokawa had visited Leyte, in the Philippines, where one of his uncles—Masamitsu's brother—had died during the war. Another brother had survived the war, going on to work for the national railway. He and his wife often hosted Shiokawa at their home, never asking for a dime and always offering a home-cooked meal. Along with Shiokawa's other surviving uncle, he had sent him a little money during high school, to help with his education. The two uncles in many ways were father figures for a young man desperate for familial connection.

When the uncle who worked for the railway died, he left behind some hair and nail clippings, which Shiokawa placed in his office safe. He plans to keep them until he finds his father and the other uncle in Leyte. Then can they finally all rest together.

The uncle who died in Leyte, Kiyotaka Shiokawa, was company commander of the 11th, in the Imperial Army's 77th infantry regiment. In 1994, Shiokawa caught wind of a memorial being planned at a temple in Yamaguchi prefecture, west of Hiroshima, for the 77th. As someone who had once yearned for more family, Shiokawa had no doubt: he'd be there. It would turn out to be a decision of fate.

Around one hundred veterans attended the service that day to honor their fallen brothers. Shiokawa was introducing himself when the man seated next to him interrupted him. He seemed incredulous.

"Are you Commander Shiokawa's son?" the man asked.

"No," Shiokawa replied, "I am his nephew. My uncle didn't have children. Did you know my uncle?"

The man's name was Katsumi Nagata. Kiyotaka Shiokawa had been his commanding officer. It was the closest Shiokawa had ever been to someone who had known a member of his family during the war.

"Did my uncle really die in battle?" Shiokawa asked the elder man.

"He died of illness," Nagata answered. He knew, because he'd been the one to bury him.

After the service, Shiokawa gave Nagata a ride home to Fukuoka prefecture. Shiokawa was convinced his uncle had brought them together and had, out of all those people in attendance, sat them next to each other. Shiokawa thought about his grandparents, who had refused to believe his uncle's death notice and had gone to their graves believing Kiyotaka was still alive. While Shiokawa was sad to be the one to confirm his uncle's

Kiyotaka Shiokawa
(courtesy Masataka
Shiokawa)

death nearly five decades after the war's end, Nagata had given him the gift of certainty. It was the same gift he wanted to provide to others.

The following year, in July 1995, Shiokawa and Nagata traveled to the Philippines to visit Leyte together. After walking several kilometers in heavy rain, Nagata stopped at the base of a hill called Mount Canguipot. This was where he'd buried Shiokawa's uncle.

For several years, Shiokawa would return to excavate around the area. Dozens of people helped him, including local residents. They expanded their search area in case heavy rains had dislodged and relocated the soil. But Kiyotaka could not be found.

Shiokawa even made a trip to North Korea in 2012. There, he excavated near the site of a former Japanese POW camp and in farmers' fields among sugarcane and pepper plants.

The Okinawa excavation tours continued until 2014. Over the course of nearly a decade, 338 people had joined Shiokawa there, from prefectures all over the country.

In addition to gathering any artifacts that appeared identifiable, Shiokawa estimates he and his fellow Japanese recovered one hundred sets of remains in total. With each finding, they gently, reverently wiped dirt from the bones using a cloth, and then placed the remains in white cloth bags. They held memorial ceremonies in the Peace Memorial Park on Okinawa—where the monument includes the names of all the war dead, regardless of nationality or which side they fought for—and placed the remains in the mortuary.

The group planned a closing event of sorts, a "tour of remembrance," in January 2015 to revisit some of the sites where they'd collected remains. But a local man named Kuniyoshi, who'd been instrumental in Shiokawa's efforts, had other ideas. There was one more place Kuniyoshi thought they should search.

That same month, Shiokawa, Kuniyoshi, and a group of volunteers descended into a passageway that had once connected the imperial forces' command bunker in Mabuni to another bunker. Shiokawa's heart raced. His father's platoon, the 116th, had at one time been connected to the command headquarters. Could this be the place?

Shiokawa dug and dug, and as he did, he prayed. He prayed that his father, Masamitsu, entombed as a thirty-one-year-old man, would "emerge from the ground," personal seal made of buffalo horn intact, and Shiokawa would know it was him. He dug and prayed, prayed and dug.

They unearthed a human tooth, communication wires, fragments of shells, and even the remains of a military horse. Masamitsu did not emerge from the ground.

"It should have been easier for the Japanese."[9]

Journalist Ian Buruma wrote those words in 1994 about Japan's postwar reckoning, and in many ways they hold true still. He continued, "The war in Asia was savage, to be sure. The sackings of Nanking and Manila, the slaves worked to death on the Thai-Burma railroad, the brutal POW camps from Manchuria to Sumatra, the millions of dead in China: these have left permanent scars on the history of Asia. But unlike Nazi Germany, Japan had no systemic program to destroy the life of every man, woman, and child of a people that, for ideological reasons, was deemed to have no right to exist."

Unlike the Nazis and the SS, there was no other name for Japanese soldiers. Perhaps that's why grappling with Japan's role in the Second World War has been both harder and easier. It seems impossible to imagine a global movement to return souvenirs taken from Nazis—to imagine signed flags of the Third Reich, emblazoned with the swastika, being packed into padded envelopes and sent back to German soil as a sign of goodwill, a gesture of peace.

But we cannot forget that the Japanese flag, for some, can and still does conjure feelings of deep pain and resentment. As Buruma wrote, the same flag that represented terror to so many, particularly in Korea and China, is still Japan's national flag. Now intended to be a symbol of international peace and human dignity, it was anything but during Japan's occupations of its fellow Asian countries.

Who were the soldiers that carried those flags into battle? We will never know the whole truth. Were some of them in Nanking, in Manila, in Burma? Did they oversee slave labor? Did they torture POWs? Did they take advantage of comfort women, the women and girls forced into sexual servitude for the pleasure of the imperial armed forces? Put more simply: Do their souls deserve to be at rest? And who decides?

Perhaps those aren't the right questions, or the wrong ones, but they aren't the only ones. Because each flag represented something else as well: a human being with a family that was left behind, without answers and mostly without institutional support of any kind. They received soul stones or abrupt death notices, which lacked an empathetic human touch, representing a cold informality that could be explained during the chaos of wartime but then was never made right. Those families sent their young men off to near-certain death in the name of an emperor and an institution and a nation that many view as having accepted little to no responsibility for the military aggression it perpetrated from the early 1900s through 1945—and also, according to Shiokawa and many others, for the institutional failures after that time. Perhaps returning the flags is more for the families, those left behind, than for the souls of the departed.

As Buruma said, it should have been easier. But a series of missteps, enabled both by outsiders, including the United States, especially during the Tokyo War Crimes Trial, and by the leaders of Japan itself, divided postwar Japan into two camps: pacifist and militarist. And the furor of both sides has made it challenging, at least publicly, for Japanese citizens to harbor viewpoints that fall anywhere in between.[10]

Shiokawa did not care much for the authorities, but his NPO was beginning to attract attention on a more official level. He often pestered officials with questions, pressing them on foggy details or missing records, furious with how the remains recovery efforts had been handled—or, in his view, neglected—for decades.

Some members of the government were open to hearing him out. For two decades, he engaged with the Ministry of Health, Labour and Welfare on remains recovery, and he had opportunities to sit in on a few hearings of the Diet, Japan's national legislature. In 2008, Shiokawa held an official briefing for members of the Diet on what he called "issues regarding the war dead."

He had distributed information ahead of time to more than seven hundred members in both houses of the Diet. On the day of the briefing, thirty-one people showed up—thirteen aides, and eighteen members themselves. At first, Shiokawa was disheartened. But he later learned it was rare for even that many members to attend a briefing by a private organization. Shiokawa was emboldened by the reaction of one of the lawmakers, who told him, "I am sorry that you are doing what the government is supposed to be doing."

In January 2011, Shiokawa sensed a potential breakthrough. Japan's prime minister, Naoto Kan, a member of the Democratic Party of Japan—a more centrist party than the conservative Liberal Democratic Party, which had been in power almost continuously since its inception in 1955—publicly declared that the long-overdue recovery of Japan's war dead was a matter of national importance and indeed the duty of the government.

Shiokawa could hardly believe what he was hearing. Finally it seemed that someone in power was taking his cause seriously. Kan increased the budget for efforts to recover the war dead, from 600 million yen to 1.6 billion yen. He pushed for a robust search on Iwo Jima, where an estimated half of the twenty thousand Japanese dead still remained. A bill was being prepared for submission to Japan's Diet.

But the bill stalled before it could get off the ground. Two months after Kan's declaration, on March 11, 2011, a 9.0-magnitude earthquake ruptured the earth beneath northeastern Japan, triggering devastating tsunamis. The subsequent disaster at the Fukushima Daiichi nuclear power plant marked the beginning of the end of Kan's term as prime minister as public outcry over the official handling of the crisis grew. By September, Kan had been replaced.

On his trips to escort home the recovered bodies of the war dead, Shiokawa would sometimes stay in the same hotel room with the remains. People would be shocked to hear it—a macabre scene, almost unimaginable. Why on earth would someone choose to stay with the bones of a dead body in their hotel room?

But Shiokawa saw it differently. It's not scary, he determined, if you think that the war dead, after all this time, are pleased to have some company.

KURUME STATION, JAPAN / MARCH 13, 2023

"How will you know what he looks like?"

Through no fault of his own, my well-intentioned husband has managed to offend me with this question as we stand in the open-air terminal of the train station, having arrived, exactly on time, from Hiroshima to meet the man who forgot we were coming.

"Of course I know what he looks like," I scoff. "I've been looking at photos and videos of him for more than a decade."

Kozue's phone rings again. She turns and looks expectantly in a certain direction, and so do we, and I'm prepared to see the man I can picture and hear in my mind. But I can't pick him out of the small crowd; even though we're all wearing masks, I had been so confident. And then there's someone on a cell phone, looking right at us. Kozue waves and hangs up.

Masataka Shiokawa is frailer, thinner, and more aged than the images of him that I've seen. The hair on the sides and back of his head is rimmed with an inch of gray, while the rest is a lighter brown than the jet-black I remember. It sits on top of the gray almost like a wig. There's white in his eyebrows and heavy bags under his eyes, all of it suggesting that the last five to ten years have not been the kindest.

It's safe to say I do not recognize him until he speaks, and then I'm sure; that gruff voice is still the same. We bow in greeting. "Shiokawa-san, arigato gozaimasu," I say. He says something to Kozue about Martin Connor-san, and I'm hit with the realization that he did not know about Marty's death. Of course not. How could he have known?

"When did Martin die?" Kozue asks me. "He wants to know."

"December 2020," I answer, and she relays. I am caught off guard that we are breaking this news to him. "He was ninety-four years old," I add, almost apologetically. "A long and incredible life."

Shiokawa turns and begins walking. We grab the handles of our rolling suitcases and follow, down the escalators and into the sun, across the street and to his car. We stuff our luggage and ourselves into his vehicle, rearranging papers and boxes and gently placing our suitcases, at his insistence, on top of more papers and boxes and a few copies of his book in the trunk.

Kozue, smaller than I and my husband, offers to sit in the middle of the backseat next to our backpacks, directing Patrick to take the front seat. Shiokawa pulls off his blue mask—COVID-19 guidelines were loosened today—but the rest of us keep ours on to be safe, in light of our recent travel. Kozue tells me that he's taking us to some kind of museum because he wants to show us a few things. It seems they are storing the material he'd been unsuccessful in returning so far.

Italian opera blares from the car stereo, and Shiokawa makes no attempt to turn it down. Kozue, already quite soft-spoken, goes to ask him a question when we notice the small hearing aid in his left ear. She leans forward and asks again, louder this time, and he grunts in response.

I have endless questions for this man, theories to check, facts to confirm, but in this moment I cannot think of a single one. It's obvious he's still processing the news that Marty is dead, and his silence fills all the gaps of the overstuffed small white car. Yet in that silence I realize my biggest theory is confirmed: Marty Connor meant more to Masataka Shiokawa than the American Marine surely ever knew.

About halfway through the drive, Shiokawa speaks again. He says something quietly, without any prompting, and Kozue gives a small gasp and looks at me. I need no further confirmation than this.

"He prays for Martin Connor every day."

Shiokawa still isn't talking much, and I'm starting to get a bit nervous. I feel the pressure of the moment, of having come all this way, of being in the car with a person I never thought I'd meet, and it's not quite going the way I'd imagined. The populated streets of Kurume have long since given way to open fields in vibrant green with orderly, neat rows. "Wheat," Shiokawa answers in Japanese when we ask what the crops are. Opera still plays on the radio.

Kozue is trying to keep any kind of conversation going, but between the loud music, being wedged in the car, the masks we're wearing, Shiokawa's hearing aid, and, I think, the news from earlier, there's not much to it. Then Shiokawa pipes up with a question of his own. "Why," he asks as Kozue interprets, "do American companies pay such high salaries?"

"Oh," I say with a little laugh. Out of everything I thought he might want to know, this was not on the list. We talk about high costs of living and health insurance. He seems intrigued and goes quiet again thinking about the answer. I try to find common ground, and remembering his childhood love of baseball, I ask if he's watching the World Baseball Classic—we plan to attend a game in a few days. He merely grunts a yes.

We pick up a few more snippets along the way. He doesn't like visiting Yasukuni Shrine because it's too political and praises the war; he prefers the national cemetery of the unknown. He's about to publish a second book in both Japanese and English, this time on wellness. He promises to send us a copy. After a lifetime of focusing on the dead, it seems he's now enamored with the living. We eventually arrive at the empty parking lot of a building that looks like an airplane hangar. The sky is clear and blue, and it is windy as we walk up the ramp to the entrance, where a sign reads, "Chikuzenmachi Tachiarai Peace Memorial Museum," with a logo of an airplane that looks like a Japanese Zero. Shiokawa opens the doors for us. "Shiokawa-san!" a few museum workers say in greeting, seeming genuinely pleased to see him. There's a small kiosk of souvenirs near the entrance. Shiokawa turns to ask me a question, which Kozue interprets: "How many children does Marty have?"

He had seven, but one son died several years ago, which is information that Shiokawa does not need at the moment. I hold up six fingers, and Shiokawa begins rummaging through the gift shop merchandise. Before I can gently remind him that we'd be more than happy to carry gifts for Marty's family on his behalf, but to please pick something small for the sake of our luggage space, a tall man in a blue museum shirt approaches to show us around.

We are standing in an area that once housed a massive military base and Tachiarai Airfield, which, according to the museum display, the Imperial Japanese Army called "the greatest airfield in the East." Young boys and men were trained here as kamikaze pilots and deployed from this base for their missions. Photos of boys, some of them no older than eleven or twelve, line the walls. We round a bend, and there's a real Japanese Zero, fully restored, one of the few that still exist. The cockpit is exactly as it was found, small and rusted and claustrophobic. The red circles on the plane's wings are striking.

Shiokawa regards it thoughtfully, inspecting the wings, and says the young people were made to die in vain. "The government bears a heavy responsibility. They truly do," he adds, as Kozue interprets. "Those with less power are always sacrificed in a war. We must not create such a world. That is my belief."[11]

We continue our tour, and Shiokawa is as interested as any of us, even though he's clearly been here before. I feel the pressure of time. We only have a few hours before we must catch a train. And I still have so many questions for this man. Also, weren't there supposed to be artifacts here, some connection to him?

There's a video, the museum guide tells us, but it's an hour long and in Japanese. We politely decline his invitation to view it. I ask about the artifacts. Kozue and the guide discuss my question. She tells us, yes, they are here.

Shiokawa had entrusted the museum with a vast archive of artifacts that he had been sent or had recovered himself over the years, but had so far been unable to return. They were not on display but preserved instead in the museum's storage area.

Our guide leads us to a large presentation room, empty except for rows of chairs and a few white tables near the front. Shiokawa is nowhere to be found. A few more museum staff come in, and we exchange greetings and business cards. They begin covering the tabletops with thin white paper, and someone rolls in a cart holding two large plastic crates. They snap open the blue lids and gently remove items, placing them on the paper-lined tables.

The artifacts, protected in plastic bags and labeled, seem endless in quantity. There are flags, canteens, photos, documents, a little green notebook that Shiokawa, who has reappeared like magic, takes an immediate interest in. More unloading onto the table: more flags, senninbari belts, hats, bits of clothing, porcelain items, fans, handwritten letters. (Shiokawa places a brown bag on the table; inside, there are tea towels adorned with Japanese planes and little individually wrapped cakes—presents, I realize, for Marty's family.)

Shiokawa is flipping through the notebook. He looks up and gestures toward the covered table in disbelief. The museum workers chuckle and remind him that *he* did all this. He remains drawn to the notebook, a liveliness about him that wasn't there

Masataka Shiokawa examines flags at the Chikuzenmachi Tachiarai Peace Memorial Museum, March 2023 (photo: Samantha Bresnahan).

before. With a cheeky grin, he takes out his cell phone and starts dialing a number that he knows by heart. He's calling the ministry, says Kozue, to ask about the name inscribed in the notebook.

"Hello, this is Shiokawa, from Saga prefecture," he declares into his phone. "I used to be involved in collection of the war dead's remains and returning of their belongings. It's been a while, and I'm old and senile now, but I still remembered your phone number. I am at the Peace Memorial Museum in Tachiarai, Fukuoka. One of the artifacts that I entrusted to them is a military handbook belonging to a Mr. Ryuichi Fukuoka. His address in in Kagawa prefecture, Mitoyo-gun in Kagawa. The Relief Division of the Kagawa prefectural office would be in charge?" He pauses, listening. "We found the military handbook and would like to return it to his surviving family." He pauses again, clearly on hold.

"They are looking to see if they can find the name," he says to the room. He seems ten years younger, vigorous, determined, alive. Everyone is curious about the call. It is a glimpse of his life, his work, happening in real time. History is alive in this room, and we are witnessing it.

He gets transferred to someone else and repeats his question. He listens again and answers more questions. "We have returned artifacts like Japanese flags, but military handbooks were the easiest to trace the origin, because the Japanese government has the records. Yes, it says Kagawa prefecture. Is there date of birth? Oh, yes, great! Date of birth is January 15, 1922." More listening, more explanations, and then Shiokawa gives his signature grunt and ends the call.

"We will call the Kagawa prefectural office," he says.

"Even with this much information?" Kozue asks him. One of the museum workers says there's a concern these days about personal data.

"They bring up personal data only when it's convenient to them," Shiokawa interjects.

Meanwhile, someone has popped the lid off another storage box, and I glance inside. It contains a manila envelope, to which is affixed a familiar return label bearing the Marine Corps logo. My heart skips: it's from Marty Connor. Shiokawa takes the envelope with a grin.

"Someone must be telling me to do this again," Shiokawa says, and the light is back in his eyes.

CHAPTER 14

Nearly three thousand miles from Syracuse, on the opposite coast of the United States, an American man named Rex and a Japanese woman named Keiko, who were engaged to be married, had an idea. At its heart, the mission would be the same as the one undertaken by Marty Connor, but this time, instead of coming from the American perspective of sending, it would come from the Japanese receiving end. Keiko's grandfather had disappeared in Burma during the war. The family had received nothing of his in return, until one day, sixty-two years later, when his flag came home. A memorabilia collector in Canada had left it with the front desk of a hotel in Tokyo; after a year of searching, the staff had found Keiko's family.[1]

The return of the flag to her family had a profound impact on Keiko, who was born in Kyoto, and on her fiancé, who was born in Oregon. There must be more Japanese battle flags that could be returned, they thought, and by 2014, the couple, by then married, had founded the Obon Society, which facilitated the return of dozens of flags to other families in Japan. (In Japan, obon is the custom of honoring one's ancestors.) Their work began while Marty was doing the same from his home in New York. Unaware of each other, they continued their endeavors from two corners of America, shipments crisscrossing, stories exchanged, a separate but shared experience of successes and failures that very few people could relate to.

The Obon Society made progress in areas Marty had never attempted, especially with the Japanese government. Still, Rex and Keiko Ziak, like Shiokawa, were met with hurdles at nearly every turn as they attempted to navigate official channels. Frustrations mounted. Resources dried up, only for the nonprofit society to be thrown a financial lifeline, allowing it to continue. The society carried on, forging a relatively small but sophisticated network of staff and volunteers across Japan.

US senators from states including Washington and California wrote official letters endorsing Obon's mission, while media coverage at both the local and national levels raised the society's profile and spread the word. Given that Japan's Ministry of Health, Labour and Welfare (MHLW) remained the gatekeeper of records, including names and addresses, in the quest to find families of the nation's war dead, the Obon Society's efforts became more difficult for officials there to ignore, especially as artifact returns mounted. In 2015, seventy years after the end of the war, Rex and Keiko traveled to Japan for an official meeting with Prime Minister Shinzo Abe.

They also lobbied eBay, the massive online marketplace, to change its policy and make the sale of Japanese battle flags a violation of the company's artifacts policy.[2] Beginning in November 2016, anyone who attempted to list "memorabilia of Japanese war dead," including flags or senninbari, received this message: "Out of respect for the personal nature of the Yosegaki Hinomaru [Good Luck] flag and the Senninbari belt to the soldiers and their families, we do not allow listings for these items. Please consider returning the item to the soldier's family." The message included a link to the webpage of the MHLW that gives information on how to return memorabilia.[3]

Masataka Shiokawa did not care for politics or politicians. Yet in his chosen line of work, dealing with the political was inescapable. It was no secret that there wasn't much love lost between Shiokawa and the authorities, particularly the MHLW. He was constantly phoning the ministry, asking for more information about this person or that, an address, a point of contact.

Move faster, he wanted to plead, time is precious. Connections to the war and to those who had died in it disappeared with each passing day, the gulf between generations becoming harder to bridge, an appreciation for the artifact and the person it represented fading into irrelevance.

Shiokawa had the MHLW on speed dial in his brain. Yet he was advised to undergo the same process that anyone contacting the ministry about an artifact would go through:

1. Application for Research is to be received by us [MHLW]. The item must bear the critical information about the original owner such as his name.

2. Using the name of the original owner as a clue, we research the personnel information our bureau has taken over from the former Japanese army and navy forces.

3. If the original owner is identified, we ask the relevant local government, where his permanent address is registered, for the whereabouts of the original owner or a family member. If they are found, it must be confirmed whether they are willing to receive the item in question.

4. If the original owner or his family member identified as above shows willingness to receive it, then we send a letter to the applicant for research asking him/her to send it to us.

5. Once we have received it, we deliver it to the local government, which takes care of the ultimate process of the return.[4]

By the summer of 2018, the MHLW claimed it had returned more than nine hundred items, most of them flags. That same year, the ministry commissioned the Nippon Izokukai (Japan War-Bereaved Families Association) to "conduct a survey on the return of the items of soldiers who fell in battle."[5] Toshiei Mizuochi, chairman of the association, noted that cooperation from the Obon Society was "essential" to fulfilling that request and wrote a letter of endorsement for the society that included a plea for more resources and support.

Mizuochi's plea was not merely political; it came from a place of personal understanding. Born two years before the war ended, he—like Shiokawa—had never "felt the warmth of a father." He knew his father, an Imperial Naval Air Corps mechanic who was killed during an air raid in the last days of the war, only from photographs.[6] He was all too aware of the scars that remained for families that were no longer complete, whose loved ones were missing.

And like Shiokawa's, Mizuochi's journey started with a trip to the battlefield. In 1974, he volunteered for a remains recovery expedition to the island of Saipan with a collective of three groups, including students, surviving veterans, and members of Nippon Izokukai. In roughly a month in Saipan, the group recovered hundreds of remains. Mizuochi and the others were shocked and angry. How could so many bodies have been left behind three decades after the war? And how many more remained out there, waiting to come home?

Mizuochi, who became a paid staff member at Nippon Izokukai, joined other search efforts—in Okinawa, Iwo Jima, Palau, New Guinea, and even Russia. He was appointed executive director of the association in 2002. He has twice visited the offices of the Obon Society in Oregon. He has seen, by his recollection, over two thousand meticulously preserved battle flags returned to Japan from across the United States and beyond.

Yet Nippon Izokukai, irrevocably tied to politics (as so many war-related entities are in Japan), is not without controversy. It was once described as an "important pressure group." Most of its members, which reportedly numbered over a million at one point in the 1990s, were known to vote for Japan's often-ruling, conservative Liberal Democratic Party.[7]

Nippon Izokukai's unassuming office is located in a building next to the National Showa Memorial Museum in central Tokyo, not far from the remnants of the Imperial Palace, and a seven-minute walk to Yasukuni Shrine, the controversial Shintō shrine largely overseen by the association. Yasukuni is said to house the souls of those who have died serving Japan since the late 1800s, particularly in the Second World War—earning, over the years, "a semiofficial stature as the national war memorial." In October 1978 Yasukuni also enshrined, in secret, the souls of convicted and executed war criminals from the Tokyo War Crimes Trial—much to the disdain of China and South Korea, whose citizens view the shrine as a memorial to Japan's militaristic, nationalist past, with support from Nippon Izokukai and its political influence.[8]

Mizuochi served as a member of the Diet's Upper House. In 2016, he helped draft a law to expand remains recovery efforts. It was not enough, he believed, for groups like Nippon Izokukai and the MHLW to be responsible for this task. It was the "responsibility of Japan as a nation."

Eight years later, Mizuochi no longer holds a government position but is still chairman of Nippon Izokukai. Some of the returned flags are stored in the association's office, and some are stored at the museum next door. They are folded and tucked into plastic bags neatly labeled with tags that read, "Obon Society." The silk, lightweight enough to carry on the body, looks fragile under the fluorescent office lighting. The group is trying to decide what to do with the flags they cannot return, either because there are no traces of surviving family members or because the relatives are not receptive to receiving the flags.[9]

Mizuochi senses the urgency of the next handful of years, as the gaps between those who personally experienced the loss of war and those who came after continue to widen. He hopes nieces and nephews and grandchildren and great-grandchildren will feel the same connection to the flags as the soldiers' siblings would have, the same sense of responsibility to preserve the legacy, to help their ancestors finally be at rest. These gestures of peace "transcend the hatred," he says.

Rex and Keiko believe that the woven strands of writing on each flag are reminiscent of DNA, each as individual as a fingerprint.[10] Thus, the Obon Society began referring to the flags as "non-biological human remains." To Rex and Keiko, the justification of the phrase was demonstrated over and over again, with every return they made. They watched as people described what it was like to feel the weight of the flag in their hands, lifting it to their face to inhale deeply, their minds conjuring a sensory memory of the hair oil their loved one wore, as if they were in the same room in that moment.[11]

The Obon Society observed American families receiving the remains of their loved ones, returned from faraway battlefields in Korea or Vietnam, and found their reactions to be identical to those of Japanese families receiving flags, senninbari, or other personal artifacts. Just as Shiokawa realized when he returned his first flag in 1999, there were other ways to bring home the lost, reinforcing Obon's mission: in lieu of bones, these objects—as personal and individual as can be—were extensions of the physical self.[12]

Sometimes, biological human remains did come back. Not because they were recovered and returned from a battlefield, but because they had been taken as a souvenir.

It sat in a homemade wooden box in the corner of Marty and Janet Connor's kitchen for a year and a half.[13] Janet could hardly stand it. It gave her nightmares. Marty didn't tell the kids. What was he supposed to say? The skull of a dead Japanese soldier was in their kitchen. It wasn't exactly normal.

The skull had arrived with a note: the veteran had originally taken it from the Piva Trail during the battle at Bougainville in 1943. His brother heard about what Marty was doing and saw a chance to finally make things right. It was similar to sentiments expressed by other Pacific veterans, many of whom sent far less chilling souvenirs to Marty's doorstep: journals and diaries, photos and letters, the famed battle flags. Some days, Marty received three or four flags in a single mail delivery. He documented the information about where and when they'd been taken and put the items in a padded mailing envelope addressed to Shiokawa in Japan.

The skull was gruesome, to be sure, but Marty, with his no-nonsense, businesslike mindset, was hardly fazed. Unfortunately, he'd seen far more than his share of body parts and bones in combat.[14] Still, before Marty could send the skull back, there was work to be done. It needed the proper resting place, and finding that turned out to be complicated. And there was something else. A derogatory phrase toward the Japanese was written in marker on top of the skull. There was no way Marty could send it back like that. The man to whom the skull belonged had suffered enough indignity. He scrubbed it using some cleaning agents he found in his laundry room.

He waited to learn how to return it to Japan. *If worse comes to worst*, Marty thought, *I'll drive over to St. Agnes cemetery on a Friday night, dig a hole, and bury it myself.*

Eventually, with Shiokawa's help, Marty shipped the skull to a contact in New York City, who obtained special permission from US Customs to personally carry it back to Japan, where he arranged to bury it in the national cemetery alongside other unidentified Japanese soldiers.

It was among Marty's trickier shipments; he did not tell the postal service employees that a human skull was inside the box. He called it an archeological artifact and hoped they would not press him any further.

The skull's homecoming resulted in some press in Japan, including attempts to identify the soldier, but his identity was never solved. Instead, the skull was given a proper burial at the national cemetery as the remains of an unknown soldier.

Rosa Ogawa, Tsunezo Wachi's daughter, knew what it was like to receive a shocking shipment through the post. Due to her father's public appeals over the years and his decision to include his home address at the end of Bill Ross's popular book on Iwo Jima, packages kept arriving from unknown senders and far-away places.[15]

Rosa's younger brother was living at Wachi's old address when one day, a large, lightweight cardboard box arrived.[16] Rosa remembered immediately sensing what it contained. Inside, a human skull stared up at them, its eye sockets vacant black holes. The only information included was that it had been found on Iwo Jima. Wasting no time, Wachi's son carefully took the skull to the MHLW to ensure it would be laid to rest in the national cemetery.

The grim delivery was a gruesome glimpse into their father's life, trapped between the realms of the living and the dead. The siblings' ability to correctly guess the box's contents underscored how deeply his endless work had permeated their own lives. After all, when you were constantly among ghosts, it was no surprise to encounter them at every turn.

CHAPTER 15

SYRACUSE, NEW YORK / 2010s

By the early 2010s, an entire solar system of support revolved around Marty's mission. Marty counted Tomoko Stultz among his friends, and the feeling was mutual. Since that day at the Syracuse airport hotel in 2004, when Sean Kirst had invited her to help translate at the meeting with Shiokawa, Tomoko and Marty had struck up a partnership.

Marty would call Tomoko and ask if he could swing by with a batch of objects for her to translate before he shipped them to Shiokawa.[1] It was a curious request—after all, Marty couldn't do much with that information, as he was unable to track down surviving family members in Japan without speaking the language or without Shiokawa. But his genuine interest made Tomoko happy to help. In fact, she felt honored.

At first, she found the whole phenomenon strange. Why had American soldiers taken the souvenirs in the first place? And why had they kept them for so long? But her work with Marty ultimately became a link to her own history that she never expected to find in Central New York, one that resulted from her befriending a man who was full of surprises and unafraid to answer her questions.

The topic of Hiroshima and Nagasaki came up between them one time. Tomoko had visited the cities and had been shocked that the atomic bombs had been dropped by the same Americans who'd passed out chewing gum and chocolate bars during the occupation. How could people do that? she'd asked Marty. How could the *Americans* have done it?

That's what war does, he'd told her. It's not you; it's what war does. Orders were orders, just or unjust. He told her the same thing about Iwo Jima. "The Japanese are the same as we are," Marty said. "They have a mom and dad, and they had to do it, as did we."

Tomoko's friend and neighbor Sean Kirst had seen Marty express that same philosophy. Sean observed that Marty never took the fighting personally. It was why Marty could withstand the emotional aftermath better than others who expressed bitter anger.[2] Marty adopted a rational, almost military-like approach: He spoke to Tsunezo Wachi at the reunion in 1970. Wachi told him that the personal artifacts meant a lot to families in Japan. Marty processed the information and set about returning the items. In the simplest terms, it was as if there were no hard feelings on Marty's part. He spoke of the Japanese with a deep respect, while others, including Sean's father, still harbored hatred for them over what had happened in the Second World War.

"Marty gets beyond that," Sean said. "And leads other people past that."

At church, a woman approached Tomoko. She had a Japanese battle flag and wanted help returning it. Tomoko connected the woman with Marty, and Shiokawa was able to find the family and return the flag. The family in Japan wrote a letter to the woman who'd returned it. Tomoko translated the letter and gave it to the woman from church. Tomoko still found these events surreal.

Besides flags and the occasional postcard, Marty brought some thousand-stitch belts to Tomoko's home, which she found the most memorable. Until a senninbari was laid out on her kitchen table, she'd never seen or heard of it. After doing some research, Tomoko was stunned at the work and care that went into each red stitch, often done by the women in the soldier's life from a place of concern, protection, and, ultimately, love.

She would translate as best she could, whether it was an old, fading postcard or names on a flag, while Marty recorded words and spellings on his yellow legal notepad. Each time he came to visit, Tomoko regarded him with admiration. And almost each time, she cried. She struggled to put into words what it meant to the Japanese people to have this man, who once fought against them, now doing something *for* them.

Tomoko reflected on everything—the histories of the two countries, the politics and brutality, the rebuilding, the treaties, the pain, the confusion, the fighting, the death. She thought about the families who had no answers and the young men haunted by ghosts. She pondered race and nationality and difference. After considering all those things and more, she decided that the old man who visited her with handfuls of history had risen above it all.

Marty Connor, she concluded, was an individual peace ambassador. "A borderless person."

Meanwhile, Marty was battling ghosts of his own making. Determined to defy aging by any means necessary, he remained fit and athletic, and Lord help anyone who dared call him old. He looked down upon the elderly and what he considered to be "old people" activities, especially senior centers, bingo nights, and certainly bowling, which he dismissed as requiring zero athletic ability.

As grandchildren began to arrive when Marty was in his fifties and sixties, he insisted they call him "Uncle Marty" instead of Grandpa (if you slipped up, you'd get "the look" and have to correct yourself).[3] In his eighties, he still dyed his hair to hide the gray, plowed the snow on his property himself (no small feat during Syracuse winters), mowed his own lawn, hunted, and skied. He even shot a wild turkey on his property to serve on Thanksgiving.[4]

He didn't want to face the fact that time was slipping by. He and Janet recognized the names of far too many friends in the obituary section of the *Post-Standard*. The passing of people from his generation also meant that the "tap," as he called it, was running dry. Originally among the younger Americans who fought during World War II, Marty was now among the oldest—and the few who survived. The veterans were dying, and with them, the stories, the memories, and the answers to some of the most basic but telling questions: how, when, where, what—and why?

Occasionally, Marty got frustrated with Shiokawa in Japan.[5] Shiokawa wasn't moving fast enough for Marty, a man who could only sleep at night if he felt confident he'd checked off every item on a mental to-do list that only he could see.[6] But Shiokawa was facing rising barriers in Japan due to increased privacy laws, which largely slowed or even outright prevented the Ministry of

Health, Labour and Welfare from releasing information to non-relatives. At a time when tracking down surviving family members was becoming increasingly urgent—as seconds and hours and days turned into weeks and months and years—the task was only becoming more difficult.

Sometimes, although Marty did not directly experience it, there were instances when Japanese families were contacted about the return of an artifact, only for the American sender to change his or her mind. Worse still, some senders asked the Japanese families to purchase back the items. Cases like these "caused a great deal of heartache and bad feelings and hurt other people's legitimate attempts to return items."[7]

"The Japanese dead still cried out for some kind of requiem," wrote renowned historian John W. Dower in 1999.[8] Shiokawa, acting as a mouthpiece for the dead, also felt like shouting, "Haven't you forgotten something?"[9] How could a country that had developed so quickly after the devastation of war simply ignore those who had made the ultimate sacrifice?

"People who died in the war cannot say that; they cannot speak," Shiokawa once said. "That's my starting point. . . . If I don't speak, who would?"

By the end of 2023, an estimated 10,590 Japanese human remains had been recovered from the place once known as Iwo Jima.[10] This number represents just half of Japan's dead on the island. There, time is also unkind; the structural integrity of the massive underground network of caves and pillboxes has become unstable, in some cases collapsing altogether, sealing those inside.

With that passing of time, another change often follows. Even the most visceral hatred can begin to flicker and weaken, eventually snuffing out, as all fires do. From the ashes left behind, clarity can arise, softening the jagged edges of hardened memories. Perhaps this change results from a personal interaction, as it did when Shiokawa met Marty and his veteran buddies. Perhaps it's through education, an understanding of how propaganda exploits the racist threads woven into societies.

Whatever the impetus, the realization is the same: our culture makes us unique, but our humanity makes us whole.

In the end, it was always about the people. The leaders who made the decisions, the individuals who carried them out. The homes in cities that were chosen for destruction and those that were spared, often by pure chance, like a tornado flattening a house and leaving the one next door untouched.

It was about the people who died and those who didn't: in the fire that rained from the skies over Tokyo, Fukui, Hiroshima, and Nagasaki; during the marches in Bataan and in the shallow waters of Pearl Harbor; from Tarawa to Peleliu, Guadalcanal, Iwo Jima, Okinawa, Midway, Leyte, Luzon, and Manila; across occupied Korea, in Nanking, China, and on the Marco Polo Bridge near Beijing; in slave-labor and POW camps in the Pacific and internment camps in the western United States.

It was always about people and power and arrogance, and in that way, the brutality of the Pacific War was no different from the wars that came before or those that would come after. What was left behind, and who, were often more significant than the material remnants—for even if a home was spared, the family might not have been. Sons, brothers, fathers, uncles, daughters, mothers, aunts.

Those who died carried objects that became extensions of themselves, and those left behind carried a void where their love resided. Sometimes the object symbolized that gap—a missing piece made whole, or at least partially so, answering questions that had burned, often for decades. Sometimes the feeling of being made whole again was an illusion of inner peace, because nothing could truly bring back the dead. But occasionally this illusion transforms into belief, and within that belief lies a healing power, one that allows the souls of both the dead and the living to be put to rest.

At an altar in Japan, a thin wisp of smoke curls from the wick of a white candle before disappearing into the air. The match used to light it is still warm to the touch. The candle's twin offers its own flame to the heavens.

At the Nagamine family altar, the man who lit the candles is bent on his knees in prayer. Masami Nagamine lost his uncle, Sadaichi, during the war, and the family knew little of what happened to him. For six decades, they had offered prayers at a butsudan that felt incomplete, lacking anything to represent the uncle's life.[11]

Then one day, Masataka Shiokawa had some news: a white T-shirt was coming from America. The T-shirt had been swiped from a backpack on the third or fourth day of the battle for Iwo Jima, on the west side of the island. It had been pocketed by Marty Connor.

Marty had tried to wear the T-shirt when he returned home to Syracuse, but it didn't fit. When he began sending his souvenirs back to Japan, he skipped over the shirt. To Marty's eye, it had no discernible identification, only a small square laundry mark penned with faded Japanese characters. He thought surely the Buddhist monk Wachi, and later Shiokawa, wouldn't be able to find anything from a laundry mark.

Sixty years later, Marty figured he had nothing left to gain by keeping the T-shirt. It served him no purpose. He had sent back most of his other souvenirs, and it was time to let this one go as well. On a whim, he tossed it into a shipment of items from other American veterans to Shiokawa. To Marty's surprise, the laundry mark included the family name.

Masami Nagamine was skeptical when a representative from the Nagano welfare department, who'd been in touch with Shiokawa, contacted him out of the blue about the T-shirt. Busy with family and work, Nagamine initially ignored the letter. A month later, the persistent officer contacted him again, assuring him that the shirt had certainly belonged to his uncle. "What do you want to do?" the officer asked.

Nagamine hesitated. But he realized the family did not even have one picture left of his father's brother. He agreed to take the shirt. Nagamine thought of his father, who had died in 1983, and wished he were alive to see this moment.

At the foot of the family butsudan, the white T-shirt now sits in a wooden frame that rests gently against the altar. A parcel tag written in Marty's hand and hanging at the neckline reads, "Shirt obtained from Japanese soldier's backpack."

After all this time, Nagamine knows his uncle's soul is finally at peace with the rest of the family. At last, the perfect fit.

EPILOGUE

WHERE ARE THEY NOW?

Shannon Moore and her husband, Tom, still live in western New York, not far from the shed she helped her mother clean out on that fateful summer day in 2003.[1] Their children are grown. Daughter Sarah is a graduate of the University at Buffalo, the same college where Professor Shimojo first translated the writing on a once-discarded ball of silk, reviving the lost memory of Jinichi Kodama, for Sarah's Veterans Day school project.

Shannon's mother, Audrey, celebrated her ninetieth birthday on May 16, 2024. Her husband, Shannon's father, Arthur Pim, who died in 1975, is laid to rest at St. Adalbert Cemetery in Lancaster, New York.

Shannon often reflects on the connection between her family and Jinichi Kodama's; on Jinichi's nephew Takao Sasaki in Fukui; on the flag that now rests alongside its brother; and on meeting the two men who made it so: Masataka Shiokawa and Marty Connor.

In Japan, Masataka Shiokawa eventually reached his limit. He felt he could go no farther. Fewer items were being returned, and even when they were, it was harder to find any surviving family members. Frustrated, aging, and tired, Shiokawa shuttered his NPO in August 2017. He, too, seemed to shut down. He gave one last interview to a Japanese newspaper and went quiet. It was why I never thought we'd have the chance to meet in person and why I was so delighted when he agreed to see us in March 2023.

Though he had helped countless families over the last half century, there remained an unfinished mission—to Shiokawa, the most important one of all. In all those trips spent searching countless caves and seeing numerous remains, he never found his father's buffalo horn. He never brought his father home.

His health had continued to decline, and he'd been dealing with a painful knee injury.[2] Shiokawa retired from his insurance business and also from the work of bringing home remains—both the physical human remains and their spiritual equivalents in object form.

Today, Shiokawa helps care for his aging wife, who has dementia. It would be another eventual parallel between his life and Marty's. And he fell in love with swimming. When we met, he was eighty and still competing in local swim meets.

Not long after our trip, Kozue sent me a message from Japan.[3] The green military notebook that had called to Shiokawa so profoundly during our visit to the museum—the one that had prompted him to phone the Ministry of Health, Labour and Welfare on the spot—had been successfully returned. The museum workers had stayed on the case for him. After Shiokawa made an official request to the prefectural office of the Nippon Izokukai, the family of the soldier who'd owned the book was found, and his nephew agreed to receive the notebook. These events unfolded thanks to our visit, the museum staff said.

Shiokawa called it something else, as if he had known all along what the result would be. He called it fate.

Tsunezo Wachi's gravesite is in a peaceful cemetery in Tokyo. On blue-sky days, when the songbirds warble, it feels like a quiet respite from the surrounding city, with only a smattering of high-rise buildings visible in the distance. Wachi's tombstone is tucked back a bit, nestled between hedges. It features two holders for flowers in front, and three tiers of stacked stones resembling steps. The tallest part of the tombstone bears an inscription on its front and left sides. Japanese characters carved into the stone cascade down the side.

Wachi's daughter, Rosa, continued her father's outreach as much as she could. She corresponded through letters, emails, and holiday cards with American families she'd met at Iwo Jima reunions through the years, her cursive script in nearly perfect English, much like her father's. On November 28, 2024, at the age of 93, Rosa passed away peacefully at home, having added her own chapter to her father's legacy of crossing old enemy lines to extend a hand of kindness and mutual respect across oceans and cultures.[4]

Marty Connor's funeral took place at the Church of St. Michael & St. Peter in Syracuse on December 10, 2020. He had lived till age ninety-four. Due to the COVID-19 pandemic, I had to watch the funeral on a livestream from my home in Georgia, unable to properly say goodbye or thank you. It was nearly ten years to the day since I had first met him. For a man whose military service framed so much of his life and who had done so much for others, it seemed unfair that this final celebration felt so muted, lacking the stirring military honors he deserved. I imagine that under normal circumstances, the small Catholic church he visited each week would have been standing-room only.

And yet, because his life centered around faith and family, perhaps the intimate setting was appropriate after all. His greatest mission had been carried out over the years without pomp or circumstance. He remained humble about his work until the end.

There were key pieces of the family missing on that day, as tragedy had not spared Marty and his loved ones. They had endured the death of a twenty-two-year-old grandson, Nathan, who died in a car accident in 2009, and the death of a son, Brian, age fifty-five, in 2014.[5]

Also noticeably absent that day was Janet. Of all the challenges Marty faced, including the war, his family says nothing tested or broke him like the decline in Janet's health. Multiple strokes and dementia had caused her to slip away from him long before he was ready to accept it. It would have been too confusing and upsetting for her to attend his memorial service. And yet, she surely knew. Just seven months later, the day after her ninetieth birthday, Janet Walsh Connor would peacefully join Marty, her hands held by their daughter Mary and son Terry as she passed from this world to the next.[6]

Marty was "determined, loyal, proud, and generous at heart," the priest told the small gathering and those of us watching on our computer screens. I thought about generosity, and kindness, and decency. Marty always said this mission of his wasn't a big deal, simply the right thing to do.

Four months later, the box from his house on the hill in Syracuse arrived on my doorstep. I placed the postcards and olive-green army pants, whose presence was almost overwhelming, in a newly purchased waterproof safe upstairs, where they bided their time on yet another stop in their journey home. The postcards were from Keith Bernard in New Orleans, Louisiana—the ones his father had picked up in Guadalcanal.

In March 2023, as my husband and I packed for our trip to Japan, I tucked the pants and the postcards, in their original envelope from Keith, into my backpack. At the Nippon Izokukai offices in Tokyo, we handed them over to the general manager, Atsushi Shigei, who promised to find out what he could about the items.

Several months later, in late July, Shigei sent me an email.[7] The postcards had been addressed to Shuichirou Kikuchi on Rota Island, in the Northern Mariana Islands. A Japanese mining company had been located there before and during the war. Shigei explained that because Kikuchi's name does not appear on any records of the war dead kept at Yasukuni Shrine, he was most likely not a soldier but a worker for the mining company. The company had ceased to exist a long time ago. It was a dead end, Shigei wrote apologetically. He offered to look after the postcards, just as he had the uniform pants we left with him and the many other items already in his care that had not yet been returned.

It was a disappointing yet realistic glimpse into the nature of this work. An answer here, twenty unanswered there. Still, helping even one family, Marty once told me, makes the effort worth it.

During Marty's funeral, I watched on my screen as Colleen stood up to deliver the eulogy for her father. "When you can count Japanese soldiers among your friends after fighting in Iwo Jima," she said with a smile, "it's fair to say you've lived an incredible life."

ACKNOWLEDGMENTS

Writing the bulk of this book during a global pandemic has been an unexpected emotional journey. I used to believe that we, as human beings, would band together in a crisis. That did not happen. I lost that faith, instead believing us to be incredibly selfish and divided. Yet this story is about the opposite. And over the course of this adventure, incredible acts of selflessness, often from complete strangers, enabled this book to come to life. In committing those selfless acts, you have all helped renew a spark of my faith in people.

A huge debt of gratitude goes to Marty Connor, his wife, Janet, and their family: Terry, Colleen, Mary, Shane, Dan, Bud, and Brian. A special, extra thank-you to Marty's granddaughter, Jessamyn Harter. Thank you all for sharing this family legacy with me.

To Shannon Moore, her husband, Tom, and her daughter Sarah, thank you for answering that phone call in 2010, and trusting me with this incredibly personal story.

This book would not exist without the kindness of Rosa Chikako Ogawa and her daughter Sophie, who so graciously welcomed us into their homes in Tokyo not once but twice. Thank you to Rosa's brother and sister-in-law, too, for the generous hospitality.

To Takao Sasaki, his wife, and his daughter Tomoko, thank you for doing the same. Masataka Shiokawa, a million thank-yous for opening up to us and allowing us into your world. Spending the day with you was something I will never forget. To the museum staff at Chikuzenmachi Tachiarai Peace Memorial Museum, thank you for everything you did that day and beyond.

Others in Japan were crucial to this project, including Natsuyo Maeda; Matsumoto Miki and Kaoru Emura from NHK; Toshiei Mizuochi, Yoko Hosogai, and Atsushi Shigei from Nippon Izokukai; Takamatsu Gushiken in Okinawa; and Yuho Tanabe at the Wakabayashi butsudan company in Kyoto.

In the United States, I extend my gratitude to Tomoko Stultz, Keith Bernard, Kath Butler and the Fifth Marine Division Association, Rex and Keiko Ziak with the Obon Society, the Iwo Jima Association of America, and author Susan Southard, who offered kindness, advice, and encouragement.

To Sean Kirst, for covering Marty's story with compassion from the very beginning, introducing readers—myself included—to his mission across Syracuse and beyond. Thank you for supporting this book.

To Yuri Davis, my never-ending thanks for agreeing to help translate material for hours on end. To production editor Melissa Veronesi, copy editor Kelley Blewster, and fact-checker Ena Alvarado, thank you all for your diligence and guidance, and for making this book so much stronger.

To my intrepid, funny, remarkable agent, Ayla Zuraw-Friedland, for making this dream come true and for always knowing exactly what I needed at any moment, and to everyone at the incomparable Frances Goldin Literary Agency. To David Black at David Black Agency for first seeing the promise of this book, and for connecting me with Joy Tutela and ultimately Ayla—thank you.

To my editor, Anu Roy-Chaudhury, a fierce advocate for this story from day one, and the entire team at PublicAffairs and Hachette: thank you for giving me this opportunity and for giving this story a platform.

Any writing about World War II benefits from the exhaustive work of scholars, historians, and journalists, many of whom are cited in this book. Thank you for the work you've done.

To my CNN colleagues who supported me every step of the way, my endless thanks: Jenni Watts, Earl Nurse, and Yoko Wakatsuki for their original collaboration on the documentary in 2010–2011; and to Elisa Berkowitz, Ellana Lee, Ryan Smith, Mike McCarthy, David Lindsay, Jonathan Hawkins, Lauren Cone, Tom McGowan, and our entire global features team. To our small but mighty original writing team, who helped get me over the finish line: Mark Tutton, Sarah Lazarus, Tom Page, Nell Lewis, and Rebecca Cairns.

Mostly, thank you to Sheri England, my biggest champion and the one who listened to my original pitch for this story in 2010, giving a young, inexperienced producer the chance of a lifetime.

This book would not exist if it weren't for the University of Georgia's narrative nonfiction MFA program, including my mentors and earliest readers, John T. Edge and Moni Basu, and my entire cohort—especially the Pulaski Street crew: KaToya Fleming, Emanuella Grinberg, Max Blau—Marty Padgett, Jeff Johnson, Mary Ann Scott, Tina Brown, Shelly Romine, Kristin Lowe, Mary White, and Mark Shavin. Thank you for shaping this story.

To Valerie Boyd, for creating that program and believing in me—in all of us—and in doing so, changing the course of our lives for the better. You continue to inspire us every day. We miss you.

To Kozue "Swasti" Oyama, a dear friend of Valerie's, for agreeing to meet us at a coffee shop in Decatur and then coming along on this wild ride without hesitation. Your selflessness and kindness continue to astonish me. From translations and phone calls to planning, emailing, texting, and being there with me for two trips to Japan, I will never be able to thank you enough for all that you've done over these many years.

I'm incredibly lucky to be supported by the most generous, kind, and encouraging friends and family. To my parents, Phil and Marianne, my sister Ali, and my bonus parents (my in-laws), John and Jane, and the entire Bresna-clan, thank you for supporting my dreams. This is as much your accomplishment as it is mine. To my grandparents, especially Pap-pap, for answering the questions of a curious high schooler all those years ago, instilling a love of history. Ashley and Amanda, thank you for keeping me sane.

To Fenway and Apollo, thanks for being the best, fluffiest writing partners a girl could ask for.

And to Patrick: my husband, my partner, my best friend, my travel buddy, my researcher, my cheerleader. My everything.

NOTES

The reporting for this book was conducted over nearly fifteen years, beginning in 2010. Information was primarily sourced from extensive in-person, phone, and virtual interviews between the author and the subjects of the book, including Marty Connor and his family, Shannon Moore, Rosa Chikako Ogawa, and Masataka Shiokawa. Other sources include original letters and documents, documentary film, photographs, home videos, and existing scholarly work on the Second World War. Wherever possible, information from interviews, which were conducted from the subjects' memories after many years had passed, was independently verified and supported with other sources. However, memory is imperfect. I have presented the most accurate version of this story to the best of my ability.

PROLOGUE
1. In 1994, Dutch author and journalist Ian Buruma wrote that as a white person in Hiroshima, regardless of your nationality (because you are often assumed to be an American visitor), "you cannot walk through Peace Park without feeling self-conscious." Buruma, *The Wages of Guilt: Memories of War in Germany and Japan* (New York: New York Review Books, 2015 [1994]), 94.

CHAPTER 1

1. Some of the details contained in this chapter are from a letter written by Masataka Shiokawa to Shannon Moore, July 26, 2004.

CHAPTER 2

1. Some of the details in this chapter come from an interview conducted by the author with Shannon Moore, February 5, 2017, and from emails exchanged between the author and Shannon Moore, June 4, 2023, and July 24, 2023.

2. G. Cameron Hurst et al., "Japan," *Encyclopedia Britannica*, last updated July 14, 2024, www.britannica.com/place/Japan; and "Amaterasu," *Encyclopedia Britannica*, accessed July 15, 2024, www.britannica.com/topic/Amaterasu.

3. Russell Kirkland, "The Sun and the Throne," *Numen* 44, no. 2 (1997), www.jstor.org/stable/3270296; T. R. Reid, "Sun Goddess Rite in Modern Japan," *Washington Post*, November 23, 1990, www.washingtonpost.com/archive/local/1990/11/24/sun-goddess-rite-in-modern-japan/41c71636-8dab-4c89-ae9a-463afe2970a0/.

4. Whitney Smith, "Flag of Japan," *Encyclopedia Britannica*, accessed July 15, 2024, www.britannica.com/topic/flag-of-Japan.

5. The Hinomaru was officially declared the national flag in August 1999, as a matter of Japanese law. "National Flag and Anthem," website of the government of Japan, accessed July 15, 2024, www.japan.go.jp/japan/flagandanthem/index.html.

6. Shoji Junichiro, "The Debate over Japan's Rising Sun Flag," National Institute for Defense Studies, November 26, 2019, www.nids.mod.go.jp/english/publication/commentary/pdf/commentary089e.pdf; Hyung-Jin Kim and Mari Yamaguchi, "Explainer: Why Japan 'Rising Sun' Flag Provokes Olympic Ire," Associated Press, July 22, 2021, https://apnews.com/article/2020-tokyo-olympics-sports-japan-japan-olympic-team-south-korea-olympic-team-5a50f35230a3330226cdc92bf4abc66d.

7. Japan's Maritime Self-Defense Force still uses the Kyokujitsu-ki, a source of tension for the country's neighbors—primarily South Korea, which views the flag as a sign of militarism from its former colonizer. "Japanese Naval Ship to Fly Rising Sun Flag at Drill in South Korea," *Japan Times*, May 26, 2023, www.japantimes.co.jp/news/2023/05/26/national/south-korea-drill-rising-sun-flag/.

8. Jürgen Paul Melzer, "Heavenly Soldiers and Industrial Warriors: Paratroopers and Japan's Wartime Silk Industry," *Asia-Pacific Journal*, September 1, 2020, https://apjjf.org/2020/17/Melzer.html.

9. "Yosegaki Hinomaru: Japanese Good-Luck Flags," National Army Museum, accessed July 15, 2024, www.nam.ac.uk/explore/japanese-good-luck-flags.

10. Details in this passage are from letters written by Arthur Pim to his sister, Bernice, dated January 3, 1945, March 14, 1945, and March 28, 1945.

11. David Vergun, "WWII Battle Helped Secure Philippines 75 Years Ago," US Department of Defense, October 23, 2019, www.defense.gov/News/Feature -Stories/story/Article/1996596/wwii-battle-helped-secure-philippines-75-years-ago/.

12. Interview with Mitsuaki Shimojo, February 12, 2018.

13. Interview with Shannon and Tom Moore, January 20, 2023.

14. Mary Pasciak, "History Hidden Away," *Buffalo News*, November 24, 2003.

15. Interview with Shannon Moore, December 2010, for the documentary film *Bridging the Pacific*, directed by Samantha Bresnahan (CNN International, originally aired May 14, 2011).

CHAPTER 3

1. Many details in this chapter come from Marty Connor's unpublished memoir, "Memories of Iwo Jima" (n.d.), and from interviews conducted with Marty Connor, son Shane Connor, son Terry Connor, and daughter Mary Harter from September 2016 to March 2017.

2. Interview with Marty Connor, December 15 and 16, 2010, for the documentary film *Bridging the Pacific*, directed by Samantha Bresnahan (CNN International, originally aired May 14, 2011).

3. Studs Terkel, *"The Good War": An Oral History of World War II* (New York: New Press, 1984), 178 (Roger Tuttrup).

4. *San Francisco Chronicle*, February 23, 1905.

5. Bradford Pearson, *The Eagles of Heart Mountain: A True Story of Football, Incarceration, and Resistance in World War II America* (New York: Atria Books, 2021), 51; *San Francisco Chronicle*, March 5, 1905, 32.

6. George Feifer, *The Battle of Okinawa: The Blood and the Bomb* (Guilford, CT: Lyons Press, 2012 [1992]), 89; Daniel James Brown, *Facing the Mountain: A True Story of Japanese American Heroes in World War II* (New York: Viking, 2021), 59.

7. Pearson, *Eagles of Heart Mountain*, 93.

8. Terkel, *"The Good War"*, 27 (Ron Veenker).

9. Gary J. Bass, *Judgment at Tokyo: World War II on Trial and the Making of Modern Asia* (New York: Alfred A. Knopf, 2023), 21; Brown, *Facing the Mountain*, 40.

10. "Executive Order 9066: Resulting in Japanese-American Incarceration (1942)," National Archives, accessed July 16, 2024, www.archives.gov/milestone -documents/executive-order-9066.

11. David Vergun, "Marines Landed on Iwo Jima 75 Years Ago," US Department of Defense, February 19, 2020, www.defense.gov/News/Feature-Stories/story/Article/2051094/marines-landed-on-iwo-jima-75-years-ago/.

12. Terkel, *The Good War,* 181 (Ted Allenby).

13. Elizabeth D. Samet, *Looking for the Good War: American Amnesia and the Violent Pursuit of Happiness* (New York: Farrar, Straus and Giroux, 2021), 116.

14. F. Tillman Durdin, "It's Never Dull on Guadalcanal: Snipers, Air Attacks, Shelling from Sea, Mud, Mosquitos All in a Marine's Day," *New York Times,* September 18, 1942.

15. George Jones, "Flame Throwers Decisive; Account for Many Pillboxes in Final Drive on Munda," *New York Times,* August 6, 1943.

16. F. Tillman Durdin, "The Battle of Buna," *New York Times,* December 29, 1942.

17. E. B. Sledge, *With the Old Breed* (Novato, CA: Presidio Press, 2010 [1981]), 64.

18. Ernie Pyle, "They Just Lay There, Blinking," April 21, 1945, column reproduced on website of Indiana University Media School, accessed August 21, 2024, https://erniepyle.iu.edu/wartime-columns/blinking.html.

19. Samet, *Looking for the Good War,* 117–124.

20. J. Glenn Gray, *The Warriors: Reflections on Men in Battle* (New York: Harper and Row, 1970), 82.

21. Document of casualties provided by Marty Connor, with casualty figures from the Personnel Department, Headquarters Marine Corps. On Iwo Jima, the Fifth Division, 26th Regiment, 1st Battalion, suffered 177 enlisted KIA (killed in action) along with four officers; 64 enlisted and two officers DOW (died of wounds received in action); and the most WIA (wounded in action).

CHAPTER 4

1. Many details in this chapter come from that memoir. Masataka Shiokawa, *To People Who Can Not Speak—Do Not Send Young People to a War Again* (Tokyo: Asahi Shimbun Publishing, 2015), chap. 2, trans. Kozue Oyama.

2. David Vergun, "Remembering the Battle of Okinawa," US Department of Defense, April 1, 2020, www.defense.gov/News/Feature-Stories/story/article/2130718/remembering-the-battle-of-okinawa/; George Feifer, *The Battle of Okinawa: The Blood and the Bomb* (Guilford, CT: Lyons Press, 2012 [1992]), 31, 109, xi.

3. James H. Belote and William M. Belote, *Typhoon of Steel: The Battle for Okinawa* (New York: Harper and Row, 1970), 24.

4. Saburō Hayashi, *Kōgun: The Japanese Army in the Pacific War*, trans. Alvin D. Coox (Quantico, VA: Marines Corps Association, 1959), 140.

5. Feifer, *Battle of Okinawa*, 90.

6. "Operation Iceberg: The Battle of Okinawa," US Army Airborne and Special Operations Museum, accessed July 16, 2024, www.asomf.org/operation-iceberg-the-battle-of-okinawa/.

7. Belote and Belote, *Typhoon of Steel*, 12.

8. Hayashi, *Kōgun*, 141.

9. David Pilling, *Bending Adversity: Japan and the Art of Survival* (New York: Penguin Books, 2014), 50. This sentiment is echoed in *Kōgun: The Japanese Army in the Pacific War*, an unflinching look at Japan's army strategy written by Saburō Hayashi, a former colonel in the Imperial Army. After 1868, Japan set out to "achieve truly advanced statehood, second to none in the world."

10. Feifer, *Battle of Okinawa*, 36.

11. John W. Dower, *Cultures of War: Pearl Harbor, Hiroshima, 9-11, Iraq* (New York: W. W. Norton, 2010), 23.

12. Mark Schreiber, "A Crash Course in Wartime Japanese Terminology for Foreign Demons," *Japan Times*, July 27, 2015, www.japantimes.co.jp/life/2015/07/27/language/crash-course-wartime-japanese-terminology-foreign-demons/; interview with Masataka Shiokawa, February 2011, for the documentary film *Bridging the Pacific*, directed by Samantha Bresnahan (CNN International, originally aired May 14, 2011).

13. Feifer, *Battle of Okinawa*, 54.

14. Belote and Belote, *Typhoon of Steel*, 70.

15. In many ways, the Battle of Okinawa took place as much at sea as on land. In fact, the relentless threat to American ships by kamikaze pilots would "rival in ferocity" the troops fighting on land. Belote and Belote, *Typhoon of Steel*, 160.

16. Belote and Belote, *Typhoon of Steel*, 252.

17. Hayashi, *Kōgun*, 141–142.

18. E. B. Sledge, *With the Old Breed* (Novato, CA: Presidio Press, 2010 [1981]), 252.

19. Studs Terkel, *"The Good War": An Oral History of World War II* (New York: New Press, 1984), 60–65 (E. B. Sledge).

20. Feifer, *Battle of Okinawa*, xi. There is widespread resentment in Okinawa against both the Japanese and American governments. Not seen as equal by mainland Japanese and subject to continued US military presence, Okinawans are trapped between two worlds. Mari Yamaguchi, "Explainer: Why Frustration Lingers in Okinawa 50 Years Later," AP News, May 13, 2022, https://apnews.com/article/japan-tokyo-world-war-ii-01228cb1c35ff2748f4cbefb1e280340.

CHAPTER 5

1. Many details in this chapter come from interviews conducted with Marty Connor, Janet Connor, son Terry Connor, daughter Mary Harter, son Dan Connor, daughter Colleen Connor, and son Shane Connor from September 2016 to October 2017.

2. Charles R. Smith, "Securing the Surrender: Marines in the Occupation of Japan," National Park Service, accessed July 17, 2024, www.nps.gov/parkhistory /online_books/npswapa/extcontent/usmc/pcn-190-003143-00/sec2.htm.

3. Letter from Marty Connor to his parents, September 27, 1945.

4. Letter from Marty Connor to his parents, September 31, 1945.

5. Honorable Discharge Certificate issued to Martin C. Connor Jr. by the USMC.

6. Shirley M. Mueller, *Inside the Head of a Collector: Neuropsychological Forces at Play* (Seattle: Lucia/Marquand, 2019).

7. K. Javed, V. Reddy, and F. Lui, "Neuroanatomy, Cerebral Cortex," StatPearls, last updated July 25, 2023, www.ncbi.nlm.nih.gov/books/NBK537247/. Also see "Cerebral Cortex," Cleveland Clinic, last reviewed May 23, 2022, https:// my.clevelandclinic.org/health/articles/23073-cerebral-cortex.

8. Mueller, *Inside the Head of a Collector*, 83, 179.

9. Lulu Miller, *Why Fish Don't Exist: A Story of Loss, Love, and the Hidden Order of Life* (New York: Simon and Schuster, 2020), 14.

10. Mueller, *Inside the Head of a Collector*, 24.

11. John Hersey, *Into the Valley: Marines at Guadalcanal* (Lincoln, NE: Bison Books, 2002), 36–37.

12. Mueller, *Inside the Head of a Collector*, 143, 103.

13. Interview with Shirley Mueller, June 15, 2023.

14. Colleen Connor recalls her mother telling a story about one of her early dates with Marty. When Marty came to Janet's house dressed in his uniform, Janet's father told her that Marty was going to get in trouble for impersonating an officer. "He always looked perpetually nineteen years old," Colleen said.

15. "Janet Connor Obituary," Syracuse.com, accessed July 17, 2024, https:// obits.syracuse.com/us/obituaries/syracuse/name/janet-connor-obituary?id =13423354.

16. Matthew Friedman, Paula Schnurr, and Annmarie McDonagh-Coyle, "Post-traumatic Stress Disorder in the Military Veteran," US Department of Veterans Affairs, June 1994, www.ptsd.va.gov/professional/articles/article-pdf /id12012.pdf.

17. Letters from Marty Connor to his family, postmarked November 15, 1943.

CHAPTER 6

1. Some of the descriptions in this chapter come from video footage taken by Marty and Janet Connor, a copy of which was provided to the author by their granddaughter Jessamyn Harter.

2. "Karl Tanner," Hall of Valor Project, accessed July 20, 2024, https://valor.militarytimes.com/hero/8337.

3. Mary E. Swain (Charles Early's daughter), "From 'Uncommon Valor' to 'Love Thy Enemy': First Reunion on Iwo Jima of Japanese & American Veterans," Fifth Marine Division Association special reunion booklet, February 19, 1970, 6–10.

4. Letter from Charles Early, July 29, 1969, reprinted in Swain, "From 'Uncommon Valor' to 'Love Thy Enemy,'" 8–9.

5. Copy of 1970 reunion itinerary, Iwo Jima Association of America (IJAA) 2018 Symposium booklet, 11.

6. IJAA 2018 Symposium booklet, 25.

7. *NBC Nightly News*, February 19, 1970 (DVD provided by the Vanderbilt Television News Archives).

8. Interview with Janet Connor, March 4, 2011, for the documentary film *Bridging the Pacific*, directed by Samantha Bresnahan (CNN International, originally aired May 14, 2011).

9. *NBC Nightly News*, February 19, 1970.

10. Dan King, *A Tomb Called Iwo Jima: Firsthand Accounts from Japanese Survivors* (Nampa, ID: Pacific Press, 2020), 121.

11. Susan Southard, *Nagasaki: Life After Nuclear War* (New York: Viking Penguin, 2015), 293.

12. Frank E. Reynolds et al., "Korea and Japan," *Encyclopedia Britannica*, last updated July 12, 2024, www.britannica.com/topic/Buddhism/Korea-and-Japan.

13. Otis Cary, "Kyōto," *Encyclopedia Britannica*, last updated July 6, 2024, www.britannica.com/place/Kyoto-Japan; "Historic Monuments of Ancient Kyoto," UNESCO, accessed July 20, 2024, https://whc.unesco.org/en/list/688/.

14. Information from interview with and materials provided by Yuho Tanabe, Wakabayashi Butsugu Mfg. in Kyoto, including the pamphlet *Kyoto Household Buddhist Altars Museum* (n.d.).

15. From NHK World documentary episode, "Kin-Butsudan: Faith Shines Brilliant in Craft That Embodies Nirvana," Art Documentaries, July 1, 2014, YouTube video, www.youtube.com/watch?v=IgmhAMbPiDc.

16. From Wakabayashi printout, "About craftsmen," n.d.; NHK World, "Kin-Butsudan."

17. "Butsudan," *Encyclopedia Britannica*, accessed July 20, 2024, www.britannica.com/topic/butsudan.

CHAPTER 7

1. Atsushi Kodera, "Master Recording of Hirohito's War-End Speech Released in Digital Form," August 1, 2015, *Japan Times*, www.japantimes.co .jp/news/2015/08/01/national/history/master-recording-hirohitos-war-end-speech -released-digital-form/.

2. Letter from Rosa Chikako Ogawa to Alfredo Cooke, April 11, 2006, reproduced in Alfredo Cooke, *Mrs. Rosa Ogawa: Her Love and Legacy for Her Warrior Dad, Captain Tsunezo Wachi* (independently published, 2023), 152.

3. Interview with Rosa Chikako Ogawa, April 12, 2018.

4. Many details in this chapter come from two unpublished accounts by Tsunezo Wachi, "Sugamo" (1977) and "August Virtue" (1989), both translated by his daughter, Rosa Chikako Ogawa.

5. Margaret MacMillan, *War: How Conflict Shaped Us* (New York: Random House, 2020), 78.

6. "Examine the Facts and Timeline of the Attack on Pearl Harbor on December 7, 1941," *Encyclopedia Britannica*, accessed July 21, 2024, www .britannica.com/study/timeline-of-the-attack-on-pearl-harbor.

7. Thomas A. Hughes et al., "Japanese Policy, 1939–41," *Encyclopedia Britannica*, last updated July 18, 2024, www.britannica.com/event/World-War-II /Japanese-policy-1939-41.

8. "Pearl Harbor: Pacific Battles," National Park Service, last updated July 26, 2022, www.nps.gov/perl/learn/historyculture/pacific-battles.htm.

9. Dan King, *A Tomb Called Iwo Jima: Firsthand Accounts from Japanese Survivors* (Nampa, ID: Pacific Press, 2020), 31.

10. Presentation by Colonel Satoshi Masaka, military attaché, Embassy of Japan, Washington, DC, at the Iwo Jima of America Association's 79th Anniversary Reunion/Symposium, Arlington, VA, February 17, 2024; Saburō Hayashi, *Kōgun: The Japanese Army in the Pacific War*, trans. Alvin D. Coox (Quantico, VA: Marine Corps Association, 1959), 79.

11. Donald Sommerville, "Battle of Saipan," *Encyclopedia Britannica*, last updated June 8, 2024, www.britannica.com/event/Battle-of-Saipan.

12. King, *A Tomb Called Iwo Jima*, 63, 75.

13. Rosa Chikako Ogawa, handwritten account, sent to the author in November 2017.

14. In 1941, because of its similarity to Pearl Harbor, Kagoshima's harbor had been used as the training ground for Japanese forces to practice ahead of their attack on the American naval base. Ronald Drabkin, "Admiral Yamamoto's Practice for Pearl Harbor: Truth and Fiction," *The Diplomat*, February 1, 2024, https://thediplomat.com/2024/02/admiral-yamamotos-practice-for-pearl-harbor -truth-and-fiction/.

15. Rosa Chikako Ogawa, handwritten account.

16. Viet Thanh Nguyen, *A Man of Two Faces: A Memoir, A History, A Memorial* (New York: Grove Press, 2023), 192.

17. "The Nuremberg Trial and the Tokyo War Crimes Trials (1945–1948)," Office of the Historian, US State Department, accessed July 21, 2024, https://history.state.gov/milestones/1945-1952/Nuremberg.

18. "Nürnberg Trials," *Encyclopedia Britannica*, last updated November 16, 2023, www.britannica.com/event/Nurnberg-trials.

19. Gary J. Bass, *Judgment at Tokyo: World War II on Trial and the Making of Modern Asia* (New York: Alfred A. Knopf, 2023), 13. According to Bass, 419 witnesses testified in court, and another 779 provided affidavits.

20. International Military Tribunal for the Far East, "Special Proclamation," January 19, 1946 (amended April 26, 1946), United Nations, www.un.org/en/genocideprevention/documents/atrocity-crimes/Doc.3_1946%20Tokyo%20Charter.pdf; "The Nuremberg Trial and the Tokyo War Crimes Trials."

21. "The Tokyo War Crimes Trials," *American Experience*, PBS.org, accessed July 21, 2024, www.pbs.org/wgbh/americanexperience/features/macarthur-tokyo-war-crimes-trials/.

22. Bass, *Judgment at Tokyo*, 6; "The People of the IMTFE," IMTFE Digital Collection, University of Virginia School of Law, accessed July 21, 2024, https://imtfe.law.virginia.edu/people.

23. Telegram, MacArthur to Eisenhower, January 25, 1946, Office of the Historian, US State Department, accessed July 21, 2024, https://history.state.gov/historicaldocuments/frus1946v08/d308.

24. "Emperor Hirohito and PM Yoshida," *American Experience*, PBS.org, accessed July 21, 2024, www.pbs.org/wgbh/americanexperience/features/macarthur-emperor-hirohito-and-pm-yoshida/.

25. Robert Trumbull, "A Leader Who Took Japan to War, to Surrender, and Finally to Peace," *New York Times*, January 7, 1989, www.nytimes.com/1989/01/07/obituaries/a-leader-who-took-japan-to-war-to-surrender-and-finally-to-peace.html.

26. Ian Buruma, *The Wages of Guilt: Memories of War in Germany and Japan* (New York: New York Review Books, 2015 [1994]), x–xi.

27. "Roster of Persons Held at Sugamo Prison as of 2400 31 May 1946," IMTFE Digital Collection, University of Virginia School of Law, accessed July 21, 2024, https://imtfe.law.virginia.edu/collections/morgan/2/3/roster-persons-held-sugamo-prison-2400-31-may-1946#expanded; Bass, *Judgment at Tokyo*, 116.

28. He later re-created the schedule in both Japanese and English in his personal notebook under the heading "Routine in jail."

29. Interview with Rosa Chikako Ogawa, April 12, 2018.

30. "Marco Polo Bridge Incident," *Encyclopedia Britannica*, last updated June 30, 2024, www.britannica.com/event/Marco-Polo-Bridge-Incident.

31. "Wachi, Tsunezo Affidavit December 23, 1946," IMTFE Digital Collection, University of Virginia School of Law, accessed July 21, 2024, https://imtfe.law.virginia.edu/collections/tavenner/5/2/wachi-tsunezo-affidavit-december-23-1946.

32. Bass, *Judgment at Tokyo*, 6–8, 10.

33. Bass, *Judgment at Tokyo*, 11.

34. "The Nuremberg Trial and the Tokyo War Crimes Trials."

35. Bass, *Judgment at Tokyo*, 623, 627.

36. Buruma, *Wages of Guilt*, 160–161.

37. "Weekly Political Notes from Japan," declassified CIA report from the US Embassy in Tokyo, April 1953.

38. Photo of certificate in a Japanese book about Tsunezo Wachi: Fuyuko Kamisaka, *Iojima Imada Gyokusaisezu* (Tokyo: Bungei Shunjū, 1993), given to the author by Rosa Chikako Ogawa and her daughter Sophie, March 2023.

39. David Vergun, "Marines Landed on Iwo Jima 75 Years Ago," US Department of Defense, February 19, 2020, www.defense.gov/News/Feature-Stories/Story/Article/2051094/marines-landed-on-iwo-jima-75-years-ago/.

40. "Former Jap Marine Honors Dead of Iwo," *Clarion Ledger*, February 4, 1952.

CHAPTER 8

1. Laurel Thatcher Ulrich et al., *Tangible Things: Making History Through Objects* (Oxford, UK: Oxford University Press, 2015), 5, 7.

2. David Carr, *The Night of the Gun* (New York: Simon and Schuster, 2008), 9, 12.

3. Thatcher Ulrich et al., *Tangible Things*, 17, 159.

4. Curiously, the date and pickup location in Wachi's return letter do not match the details from Marty's first letter. It is possible that Marty sent a second letter and shipment, but that is unlikely in such a short span of time. It is also possible that Wachi, juggling countless correspondences, made an error in his reply. But even that is out of character for a man whom his daughter described as a perfectionist, a man who sometimes went as far as trying to intercept letters at the post office after he sent them in an attempt to fix even the smallest mistake. The explanation, it seems, is lost to history.

5. Many details in this chapter come from Masataka Shiokawa's memoir, *To People Who Can Not Speak—Do Not Send Young People to a War Again* (Tokyo: Asahi Shimbun Publishing, 2015), chap. 2 (trans. Kozue Oyama) and chap. 4 (trans. Yuri Davis).

6. US Defense POW/MIA Accounting Agency, *World War II: Europe-Mediterranean Directorate*, n.d., page 2, www.dpaa.mil/Portals/85/EM%20World%20War%20II.pdf.

7. David Vergun, "DOD Still Seeks to Find Missing Service Members from World's Battlefields," US Department of Defense, September 17, 2021, www.defense.gov/News/News-Stories/Article/Article/2774347/dod-still-seeks-to-find-missing-service-members-from-worlds-battlefields/.

8. Email to the author from Satoshi Masaka, military attaché, Embassy of Japan, February 23, 2024, citing the most recent numbers from the Ministry of Health, Labour and Welfare (MHLW). Total killed in action: approximately 2,400,000. Already collected: approximately 1,277,000. Still missing: approximately 1,123,000.

9. "Request for Information Regarding the Remains of War Dead in Sunken Ships," Embassy of Japan, accessed July 22, 2024, www.mh.emb-japan.go.jp/files/100095146.pdf.

10. Email to the author from Naohiro Manago, attaché for MHLW, Embassy of Japan, March 5, 2024.

11. "Chidorigafuchi National Cemetery," Japanese Ministry of the Environment, accessed July 22, 2024, www.env.go.jp/garden/chidorigafuchi/1_intro/index.html.

12. Collin Rusneac, "Building Transnational Memories at Japanese War and Colonial Cemeteries," *Asia-Pacific Journal*, May 15, 2022, https://apjjf.org/2022/10/rusneac.

CHAPTER 9

1. This passage is based on correspondence between Tsunezo Wachi and Marty Connor dated March 23, 1984, May 30, 1984, November 29, 1984, and December 12, 1984.

2. Interview with Marty Connor, October 14, 2017.

3. Dan King, *A Tomb Called Iwo Jima: Firsthand Accounts from Japanese Survivors* (Nampa, ID: Pacific Press, 2020), 202.

4. Some details in this passage come from interviews conducted with Rosa Chikako Ogawa, November 17, 2017, and April 12, 2018.

5. Email to the author from Kozue Oyama, November 6, 2017, who spoke to Rosa Ogawa by phone on the author's behalf.

6. Letter from Rosa Ogawa to Alfredo Cooke, August 19, 1995, reproduced in Alfredo Cooke, *Mrs. Rosa Ogawa: Her Love and Legacy for Her Warrior Dad, Captain Tsunezo Wachi* (independently published, 2023), 8.

7. Interview with Marty Connor, November 11, 2016.

CHAPTER 10

1. Many details in this chapter come from an interview with Shannon Moore, February 5, 2017, and from an email from Moore to the author, February 5, 2017.

2. Interview with Mitsuaki Shimojo, February 12, 2018.

3. Some details in this chapter come from Sean Kirst, "Reverence for Japanese War Veterans Reverberates," *Post-Standard* (Syracuse), April 30, 2004, and from a 2011 interview with Sean Kirst for the documentary film *Bridging the Pacific*, directed by Samantha Bresnahan (CNN International, originally aired May 14, 2011).

4. Some details in this chapter come from the documentary *Hinomaru* (NHK, 2004), VHS.

5. Many details in this chapter come from Masataka Shiokawa, *To People Who Can Not Speak—Do Not Send Young People to a War Again* (Tokyo: Asahi Shimbun Publishing, 2015), chap. 4 (trans. Yuri Davis), and from an interview with Shiokawa in February 2011 for *Bridging the Pacific*.

6. Chiang Yee, "Japanese Calligraphy," *Encyclopedia Britannica*, last updated August 11, 2023, www.britannica.com/art/Japanese-calligraphy.

7. "Japanese Calligraphy," Japan-Guide.com, accessed July 23, 2024, www.japan-guide.com/e/e2095.html.

8. Obituary of Raymond Salvie, *Post-Standard* (Syracuse), September 3–4, 2022, https://obits.syracuse.com/us/obituaries/syracuse/name/raymond-salvie-obituary?id=36409711.

9. Interview with Tomoko Stultz, October 15, 2017.

10. Copy of email from Naomi Tanaka supplied to the author by Shannon Moore. She received it at 8:43 p.m. on Thursday, June 3, 2004.

CHAPTER 11

1. Some information in this chapter comes from email correspondence from Tomoko Sasaki to the author, October 19, 2023.

2. Many details in this chapter come from an interview with Takao Sasaki, March 2023, trans. Yuri Davis.

3. Letter from Moore family to Kodama family, hard copy courtesy of Takao Sasaki. Shannon Moore provided a digital copy of the same letter; in it, the word "Grandfather" is used in place of "Uncle."

4. Copy of email shared with author, originally received by Shannon Moore on July 7, 2004.

5. Email sent by Shannon Moore via her husband Tom's email address to Takao Sasaki, July 11, 2004. Hard copy also provided by Takao Sasaki.

6. Interview with Shannon Moore, December 2010, for the documentary film *Bridging the Pacific*, directed by Samantha Bresnahan (CNN International, originally aired May 14, 2011).

7. Copy of letter from Masataka Shiokawa to Shannon Moore, provided to the author by Shannon.

8. Email to the author from Kozue Oyama, June 25, 2020, after speaking to Takao Sasaki over the phone on the author's behalf.

CHAPTER 12

1. "Iwo Jima," *Encyclopedia Britannica*, last updated July 16, 2024, www .britannica.com/place/Iwo-Jima-island-Japan; "Iwo Jima: Return of a Battlefield," *Time*, April 5, 1968, https://time.com/archive/6835041/iwo-jima-return-of -a-battlefield/.

2. Interview with Marty Connor, October 14, 2017.

3. Marty Connor, interview on Iwo Jima by Mike Chinoy, March 2005, accessed in the CNN archive.

4. "Teddy Draper, Sr.," Library of Congress, accessed July 24, 2024, https:// guides.loc.gov/navajo-code-talkers/profiles/teddy-draper.

5. Keith Pannell, "Code Talker Describes Military Experience," US Air Force, November 29, 2004, www.af.mil/News/Article-Display/Article/135504 /code-talker-describes-military-experience/.

6. "Marine Corps Updates Its Official Records of First Flag Raising over Iwo Jima," press release, US Marine Corps, August 24, 2016, www.marines .mil/News/Press-Releases/Press-Release-Display/Article/924206/marine-corps -updates-its-official-records-of-first-flag-raising-over-iwo-jima/; Thomas Clouse, "Code Talkers' Secret Helped Win War," *Spokane Spokesman-Review*, July 26, 2002, www.spokesman.com/stories/2002/jul/26/code-talkers-secret-helped-win -war-language-saved-/; Ted Draper, interview on Iwo Jima by Mike Chinoy, aired on *Lou Dobbs Tonight*, "A Tribute to Heroes," May 30, 2005.

7. David Vergun, "Marines Landed on Iwo Jima 75 Years Ago," US Department of Defense, February 19, 2020, www.defense.gov/News/Feature -Stories/story/Article/2051094/marines-landed-on-iwo-jima-75-years-ago/.

8. Letter from Rosa Ogawa to Alfredo Cooke, July 27, 2005, reproduced in Alfredo Cooke, *Mrs. Rosa Ogawa: Her Love and Legacy for Her Warrior Dad, Captain Tsunezo Wachi* (independently published, 2023), 138. Certain other details in this chapter come from this source, as well as from correspondence between Rosa Ogawa and Marty Connor dated December 18, 1999, September 14, 2004, and December 14, 2004.

9. Rosa Ogawa's birthday is March 27, 1931.

10. For a look at some of Rosa's correspondence with another USMC veteran (not of WWII but later), see Cooke, *Mrs. Rosa Ogawa*.

11. Exchange captured on camera by CNN crew, March 2005, accessed in the CNN archive.

12. In a letter to his parents from Camp Pendleton, March 25, 1944, Marty joked, "How's the old homestead getting on without its most prized possession, mainly me?" Other details in this passage come from interviews with Marty Connor, son Terry Connor, daughter Mary Harter, January 28, 2017, and with daughter Colleen Connor, September 7, 2023.

13. Obituary of J. Robert Cudworth, Buranich Funeral Home, July 2013, https://www.buranichfuneralhome.com/obituaries/j-robert-cudworth.

14. Interview with Bob Cudworth, December 2010, for the documentary film *Bridging the Pacific*, directed by Samantha Bresnahan (CNN International, originally aired May 14, 2011).

15. Colleen Connor mentioned that her father thought Janet, an avid reader, was much smarter than he, and that he'd struggled with reading in school.

16. Peter Applebome, "Relics of Iwo Jima, Bound for Home," *New York Times*, May 30, 2004; *Bridging the Pacific*.

17. Interview with Sean Kirst, March 4, 2011, for *Bridging the Pacific*.

18. The following emails and letters were all found in Marty Connor's files.

19. Some details in this passage come from an interview with Keith Bernard, February 15, 2022.

20. Copy of newspaper clipping provided by Keith Bernard.

21. Translation of postcards by Kozue Oyama.

CHAPTER 13

1. Translation and field notes from CNN Tokyo producer Yoko Wakatsuki, February 10, 2011, for the documentary film *Bridging the Pacific*, directed by Samantha Bresnahan (CNN International, originally aired May 14, 2011).

2. Some details in this chapter come from interviews with Torao Shizuka and Masataka Shiokawa, February 10, 2011, trans. Yoko Wakatsuki, for *Bridging the Pacific*.

3. This and certain other details in the chapter come from Masataka Shiokawa, *To People Who Can Not Speak—Do Not Send Young People to a War Again* (Tokyo: Asahi Shimbun Publishing, 2015), chap. 2 (trans. Kozue Oyama) and chap. 4 (trans. Yuri Davis).

4. "Operation Iceberg: The Battle of Okinawa," US Army Airborne and Special Operations Museum, accessed July 28, 2024, www.asomf.org /operation-iceberg-the-battle-of-okinawa/.

5. Some details in this chapter come from an interview with Takamatsu Gushiken in Okinawa, April 17, 2018, trans. Kozue Oyama.

6. Matthew M. Burke and Chiyomi Sumida, "Bone Collector: Nonprofit Dedicated to Recovering WWII Remains in Okinawa," *Stars and Stripes*, October 6, 2015.

7. "Dozens of Bones Found in Planned Dirt Excavation Site in Komesu, Itoman, Says Okinawa Prefecture and War-Dead Remains Recovery Group," *Ryukyu Shimpo*, February 26, 2021, trans. T&CT and Sam Grieb, https://english .ryukyushimpo.jp/2021/03/02/33433/.

8. "War Remains Recovery Volunteer Touts Importance of Keeping Battle of Okinawa Lessons Alive," *Ryukyu Shimpo*, September 25, 2017, trans. T&CT and Erin Jones, https://english.ryukyushimpo.jp/2017/09/29/27790/.

9. Ian Buruma, *The Wages of Guilt: Memories of War in Germany and Japan* (New York: New York Review Books, 2015 [1994]), ix.

10. David Pilling, *Bending Adversity: Japan and the Art of Survival* (New York: Penguin Books, 2014), 222–223:

> Japan will never stop its wartime apologists, just as Germany cannot hope to silence its neo-Nazis. But conservatives and nationalists have tended to dominate the discourse in Japan, overshadowing the statements and actions of many Japanese who have sought to look at history more squarely. As a result, the revisionist view of history is often seen by Japan's critics as the true sentiments of its people, normally hidden but revealed after a few glasses of sake or in the company of fellow Japanese. The rightwing has certainly kept alive the idea that Japan's was an honourable war of national defence and Asian liberation fought against western colonial aggression. Sure, the Imperial Army did terrible things, some will admit. But wasn't that the nature of war?

11. Interview with Masataka Shiokawa, March 13, 2023, trans. of transcript by Yuri Davis.

CHAPTER 14

1. Website of the Obon Society, accessed July 28, 2024, https://obonsociety .org/eng/page/history.

2. KiMi Robinson, "Oregon-Based Group Works to Heal Wounds of WWII with Flag Returns," Kyodo News, July 21, 2018, https://english.kyodonews .net/news/2018/07/4095c26ee3cf-feature-oregon-based-group-works-to-heal -wounds-of-wwii-with-flag-returns.html#google_vignette.

3. Email to the author from Scott Overland, eBay Corporate Communications, November 13, 2023.

4. Email to the author dated June 21, 2018, from MHLW's Ms. Matsudo, Investigation Group #3, Planning Division of Recovery of the Remains of War Dead, Social Welfare and War Victims' Relief Bureau.

5. Facsimile of letter from Nippon Izokukai endorsing the Obon Society, December 14, 2018, https://obonsociety.org/uploads/2020/06/11/Izokukai _Endorse.jpg.

6. Some details in this chapter come from an interview with Toshiei Mizuochi, March 7, 2023, trans. Yuri Davis. Biographical information provided to the author by Nippon Izokukai, March 2023. Nippon Izokukai was founded in 1947, during the American occupation of Japan.

7. Ian Buruma, *The Wages of Guilt: Memories of War in Germany and Japan* (New York: New York Review Books, 2015 [1994]), 220.

8. Gary J. Bass, *Judgment at Tokyo: World War II on Trial and the Making of Modern Asia* (New York: Alfred A. Knopf, 2023), 671–672.

9. Interview with Atsushi Shigei at the offices of Nippon Izokukai, March 7, 2023.

10. "Non-biological Human Remains," Obon Society, accessed July 28, 2024, https://obonsociety.org/eng/page/non-biological-human-remains.

11. Interview with Rex and Keiko Ziak, February 17, 2023.

12. If you are interested in returning World War II items taken from Pacific battlefields to Japan, please contact the nonprofit Obon Society, located in Astoria, Oregon, USA, https://obonsociety.org/eng/ (English) or https://obonsociety.org /jpn (Japanese).

13. Some details in this passage come from interviews with Marty Connor, January 27, 2017, and October 14, 2017.

14. Interview with Marty Connor, December 2010, as part of the documentary film *Bridging the Pacific*, directed by Samantha Bresnahan (CNN International, originally aired May 14, 2011).

15. Bill D. Ross, *Iwo Jima: Legacy of Valor* (New York: Vintage Books, 1985).

16. Interview with Rosa Ogawa, April 12, 2018.

CHAPTER 15

1. Some details in this chapter come from interviews with Tomoko Stultz, March 6, 2017, and October 15, 2017.

2. Interview with Sean Kirst, January 28, 2017.

3. Interview with Colleen Connor, daughter of Marty Connor, March 7, 2017; interview with Jessamyn Harter, granddaughter of Marty Connor, March 12, 2017.

4. From Colleen Connor's eulogy of her father, delivered at his funeral

on December 10, 2020; Facebook post by his granddaughter, Jessamyn Harter, December 4, 2023.

5. Interview with Marty Connor, January 27, 2017.

6. Interview with Shane Connor, son of Marty Connor, March 10, 2017.

7. Dan King, "Returning WWII Souvenirs," *Black Sands* (newsletter of the Iwo Jima Association of America), Summer 2011, 7.

8. John W. Dower, *Embracing Defeat: Japan in the Wake of World War II* (New York: W. W. Norton, 1999), 486.

9. Interview with Masataka Shiokawa, February 10, 2011, trans. Yoko Wakatsuki (CNN Tokyo producer), as part of the documentary film *Bridging the Pacific*, directed by Samantha Bresnahan (CNN International, originally aired May 14, 2011).

10. Presentation by Colonel Yuka Nanazato, military attaché, Embassy of Japan, Washington, DC, at the Iwo Jima of America Association's 79th Anniversary Reunion/Symposium, Arlington, VA, February 17, 2024.

11. Field notes from CNN Tokyo producer Yoko Wakatsuki during interview with Masami Nagamine, February 11, 2011, for *Bridging the Pacific*.

EPILOGUE

1. Email to the author from Shannon Moore, April 30, 2024.

2. Interview with Masataka Shiokawa on March 13, 2023.

3. Email to the author from Kozue Oyama, May 8, 2023.

4. Message to the author from Rosa's daughter, Sophie, January 10, 2025.

5. "Nathan Harter Obituary," Syracuse.com, August 28, 1999, https://obits .syracuse.com/us/obituaries/syracuse/name/nathan-harter-obituary?id=49208366; "Brian Connor Obituary," Syracuse.com, June 23, 2014, https://obits.syracuse.com /us/obituaries/syracuse/name/brian-connor-obituary?id=23059295.

6. "Janet Connor Obituary," Syracuse.com, July 20, 2021, https://obits .syracuse.com/us/obituaries/syracuse/name/janet-connor-obituary?id=13423354.

7. Email to the author from Atsushi Shigei, July 19, 2023.

INDEX

Samantha Bresnahan is a supervising producer for CNN International, based in London. She's reported across the US and around the world, producing global features from India, Brazil, Japan, Kuwait, Thailand, South Korea, Jamaica, Norway, England, Hong Kong, France, the United Arab Emirates, and beyond. She is a four-time News and Documentary Emmy Award nominee, a Livingston Award finalist, and winner of multiple National Headliner Awards. In addition to her more than fifteen years of experience as a journalist, Bresnahan holds a master of fine arts degree in narrative nonfiction from the University of Georgia.

PublicAffairs is a publishing house founded in 1997. It is a tribute to the standards, values, and flair of three persons who have served as mentors to countless reporters, writers, editors, and book people of all kinds, including me.

I. F. STONE, proprietor of *I. F. Stone's Weekly*, combined a commitment to the First Amendment with entrepreneurial zeal and reporting skill and became one of the great independent journalists in American history. At the age of eighty, Izzy published *The Trial of Socrates*, which was a national bestseller. He wrote the book after he taught himself ancient Greek.

BENJAMIN C. BRADLEE was for nearly thirty years the charismatic editorial leader of *The Washington Post*. It was Ben who gave the *Post* the range and courage to pursue such historic issues as Watergate. He supported his reporters with a tenacity that made them fearless and it is no accident that so many became authors of influential, best-selling books.

ROBERT L. BERNSTEIN, the chief executive of Random House for more than a quarter century, guided one of the nation's premier publishing houses. Bob was personally responsible for many books of political dissent and argument that challenged tyranny around the globe. He is also the founder and longtime chair of Human Rights Watch, one of the most respected human rights organizations in the world.

.   .   .

For fifty years, the banner of Public Affairs Press was carried by its owner Morris B. Schnapper, who published Gandhi, Nasser, Toynbee, Truman, and about 1,500 other authors. In 1983, Schnapper was described by *The Washington Post* as "a redoubtable gadfly." His legacy will endure in the books to come.

Peter Osnos, *Founder*